TALES FROM THE
GALLEY

STORIES OF THE WORKING WATERFRONT

Other Books by Doreen Armitage

Around the Sound: A History of Howe Sound—Whistler

Burrard Inlet: A History (finalist for the 2002 City of Vancouver Book Award)

From the Wheelhouse: Tugboaters Tell Their Own Stories (finalist for the 2004 BC Booksellers' Choice Award)

TALES FROM THE GALLEY

STORIES OF THE WORKING WATERFRONT

Doreen Armitage

HARBOUR PUBLISHING

Published by Harbour Publishing Co. Ltd., P.O. Box 219, Madeira Park,
BC V0N 2H0
www.harbourpublishing.com

Page Design by Warren Clark
Cover Photo by Boomer Jerritt
Half-title page photo courtesy of University of British Columbia Library,
Rare Books and Special Collections, Fishermen Publishing Society,
#1532-477-1

Printed and bound in China

Harbour Publishing acknowledges the financial support from the
Government of Canada through the Book Publishing Industry
Development Program (BPIDP) and the Canada Council for the Arts,
and the Province of British Columbia through the British Columbia Arts
Council, for its publishing activities.

Library and Archives Canada Cataloguing in Publication

Armitage, Doreen, 1931–
    Tales from the galley : stories of the working waterfront / Doreen
Armitage.

Includes index.
ISBN 978-1-55017-438-0

    1. Navigation—British Columbia—Pacific Coast—History.
2. Seafaring life—British Columbia—Pacific Coast—History. 3. Pacific
Coast (B.C.)—History. 4. Oral history. I. Title.

VK139.A758 2007   387.509711'1   C2007-903875-1

Contents

To Bill

. . . with love.

ACKNOWLEDGEMENTS

I extend my deep appreciation to the men who shared their maritime experiences with me. Most were mariners, from fishermen to pilots, from Coast Guard officers to tugboaters. Some were divers, others were oil drilling rig workers tasting the Pacific's awesome power for the first time. They all are brave and adventurous people whose jobs called for as much as they could give and more.

I would also like to acknowledge the help of Clinton Tippett, geology advisor for Shell Canada Limited, whose unfailing cooperation enabled me to locate former employees and share the history of the *Sedco 135F*, Canada's first oil drilling rig.

Thank you, gentlemen.
Doreen Armitage

Previous page: Aboard the *Northern Dawn*, skipper George Olafson swaps stories with the skipper of the *Leslie Ellen* during a 1988 herring opening in Cypress Bay, near Tofino.
Brian Gauvin photo

Introduction

The stories in this book recount actual events experienced by the men sharing them, oral histories from still-working and retired mariners, men who have experienced much of what nature has to offer on the sea.

During my interview with one of the seamen, he mused, "You know, Doreen, people really don't know what goes on out there." Very true. Hopefully these personal stories will provide some insight into what does go on in the lives of those who earn their livelihood in and on the ocean.

Pulling in a haul, it's hard to tell who's more appreciative of the catch, the fishermen or the seagulls.

City of Richmond Archives, photograph #1985 0004 00112[1]

BC's first fish cannery opened in 1867, and by the 1920s production lines were producing as many as two million cases of salmon annually—most of which were exported to Britain. With the advent of refrigeration technology, canneries were phased out and frozen-fish processors became the norm.
Harbour Archives

Around the same time as the British government built British Columbia's first light station in 1860, skippers of sailing ships recognized the need for pilots to give their advice in traversing unfamiliar waterways, with their dangerous tidal rips and hidden rocks. As settlers arrived on the coast the lumber mills proliferated, along with their need for steam-powered tugboats to transport logs. From lone fishermen supplying their families' needs, the fishing industry expanded, eventually involving trollers, seiners, gillnetters and packers. Many fishermen were, and still are, lost at sea, their boats unable to withstand the ravaging storms. In time, besides fishing from boats, a whole new industry developed—dive fishing for shellfish and their roe, underwater harvesting.

With Canada's great offshore bounty, the need arose for federal regulations to control fishing in Canadian waters. The government developed offshore fishing zones, and Fisheries boats patrolled and helped regulate catches. Assistance was needed for foundering and damaged vessels and their crews, and the Canadian Coast Guard was formed with its prime focus on providing Search and Rescue services.

The first venture beneath Canadian waters came with a Shell oil-drilling rig off Vancouver Island's west coast, after several years of geological research. The rig drilled core samples for two years between 1967 and 1969.

This book is the story of the people involved, told largely in their own words. The tales of the sea are as varied as life itself and, as you will see, often much more unbelievable.

British Columbia

Dixon Entrance

Nass River

Langara Island
(Lacy Island)

Port Simpson

Prince Rupert

Masset Inlet

Kitimat

Queen
Charlotte
Islands

Grenville Channel

Banks Island

Cumshewa Inlet

Hecate Strait

Tasu

Bonilla Point

Aristazabel Island

Bella Bella

Ocean Falls

Principe Channel

(Cape St. James)

Inside Passage

Namu

Hakai Pass

Queen Charlotte Sound

Cape Scott

Coal Harbour

Port Hardy

Winter Harbour

Quatsino Sound

Alert Bay

Port McNeill

Quadra Island

Cape Cook

Kyuquot Sound

Tahsis

Esperanza Inlet

Vancouver Island

Texada Island

Agamemnon Channel

Nootka Island

Nootka Sound

Comox

Pender Harbour

Gold River

Howe Sound

Bowen Island

Clayoquot Sound

Port Alberni

False Creek

Qualicum

Vancouver

Tofino

Nanaimo

Ladysmith

Barkley Sound

Mayne Island

Saltspring Island

Saturna Island

Strait of Georgia

Fraser River

Bamfield Inlet

Port Renfrew

Esquimalt

Victoria

Juan de Fuca Strait

Pacific Ocean

N

0   100 km

0   100 Miles

Strait of Georgia

Gambier Island

Howe Sound

Bowen Island

Vancouver Harbour
(English Bay)

Vancouver

Sea Island

Richmond

Roberts Bank

Steveston

Sand Heads

Boundary Bay

CHAPTER ONE

A Queer Wave and Herring Sets

Commercial Fishing

"Someone asked me, 'How much fish can that boat pack?' and I said that we could probably get about sixty tons on it but it wouldn't float. It was an old boat—just a piece of junk. We started loading what we could pack, and meantime this helicopter from the Compensation Board was flying right around us. Our picture appeared in an article in their magazine that came out later. The caption said, 'That's what an overloaded herring vessel looks like.' It didn't look too good."

Fisherman Gordie Stanley

(left) The *Prosperity*, Byron Wright's third fishboat, is photographed on sea trials in Indian Arm, February 1990. It's a life of great moments, the occasional million-dollar day and priceless views.
Courtesy Byron Wright

Like so many boats that were named in honour of loved ones, Gordie Stanley's twelve-metre (forty-foot) troller, the *Miss Toni*, was named after his daughter.
Gordie Stanley photo

Commercial fishing in British Columbia began during the fur trade period in the early nineteenth century but expanded dramatically after 1870 when salmon canneries were established at the mouth of the Fraser River and a few years later at the mouth of the Skeena. Although the province would later profit from substantial fisheries in sardines, herring and halibut, salmon accounted for two-thirds of the dollar value of the fishing industry in this province until the 1920s. Management of the salmon fishery, however, has always been complicated by the fact that some salmon stocks hatched in Canada enter US waters and some hatched in the US enter Canadian waters. A first treaty between the two countries to deal with this issue was signed in 1937. It was superseded by the Pacific Salmon Treaty in 1985.

Commercial fisherman Gary Robinson gaffs a halibut in Hecate Strait.

Brian Gauvin photo

Halibut have been commercially fished in British Columbia since the 1880s. The larger ones, such as this catch aboard the *Andrew Kelly* in 1915, can weigh as much as 270 kilograms

City of Richmond Archives, photograph #1985 4 880

"In the 1950s we had no agreement with the Americans about pink salmon," fisheries economics specialist and part-time fisherman Don Pepper explains, "although we had a sockeye agreement that split those going through Juan de Fuca between us. The Fisheries minister at that time, Jimmy Sinclair, wanted a pink salmon treaty with the Americans, but they wouldn't come to the negotiating table. However, it happened that the Canadian fishing fleet had bought a whole lot of sardine boats from the Americans after the collapse of

Overloaded boats, sadly, are not just a thing of the past.

Vancouver Public Library Special Collections, VPL 10402A

their fishery, so Mr. Sinclair allowed them to fish on the west coast with the objective of catching as many pinks as possible to force the Americans to the bargaining table. When the Americans saw that the Canadian fleet could catch all the pink salmon, they agreed to come to the table and we signed a Fraser River pink salmon agreement. They instituted the Blue Line, running from Bonilla Point, just below Carmanah Point, to Tatoosh Island, and Canadians could only fish behind it to the east. All the boats would line up at the Blue Line and pick their setting spots with the length of a net between the various boats. You would set your net at the ebb tide, but you had to be closed up by the time you were at the Blue Line because Fisheries boats like the *Tanu* would be patrolling there. It worked very well."

Changes in the management of BC's herring fishery reflect the gradual accumulation of knowledge about the life cycle of this species and its conservation. A reduction fishery, begun in the 1930s to make fishmeal for chicken feed, was abruptly cancelled in 1967 when stocks failed; a herring fishery begun in 1972 catered to the Japanese sushi market but used only the roe. "These days," says veteran fisherman Gordie Stanley, "the whole herrings go to the fish plants at Prince Rupert or Steveston, the roe is removed and sold to Japan and the herring carcasses are processed into mash and oil. They make fertilizer out of the mash." The oil is used as a supplement in feed for animals.

At one time, drying nets seemed as endless as the resources they caught. Early linen nets required much care and mending, but provided for plenty of yarn-spinning around the net floats.
Vancouver Public Library Special Collections, VPL 18695

(right) A purse seiner brings in a herring catch in Barkley Sound. Most herring roe is destined for the Japanese sushi market, and the carcasses are processed into fertilizers or animal food.
Brian Gauvin photo

There is now a fishery for dogfish, although Don Pepper points out that "you don't make much money at it. You set individual baited hooks and bring them up one fish at a time. You don't have to clean them, but dogfish have a curious inability to urinate. They secrete the urea through the skin—that's where they get that dirty diaper smell—so you want to get them to the plant within three days so the urea doesn't get into the flesh."

There is also a new fishery for Pacific sardines, commonly called pilchards. Sardines dominated West Coast fisheries from 1925 to 1946, keeping fifteen reduction plants in business, but stocks collapsed in

1947 from overfishing and unfavourable environmental conditions. In the early 1990s sardine stocks began to rebound and in 1999 the first large scale test fishery was held off the west coast of Vancouver Island. "Since then," Don Pepper continues, "we've had over 100,000 metric tonnes of sardines in BC waters, and we have had a total allowable annual catch of 15,000 metric tonnes. Twenty-seven boats fished them in 2004. The fish come up from California and Oregon to feed, usually in late June and July, and stay until November when the water temperatures change and they go south again to spawn. There are two markets for them—the biggest fish go to the food market and the smaller ones go to the bait market for the Taiwanese, Japanese and Korean high seas longline tuna fleets. The world market is maybe 80,000 metric tonnes. The price for the tuna bait is fixed worldwide. The price for food fish is much higher but the markets are very small, although they are opening up. The Japanese sardine industry has collapsed, so we have a food market there and in the Ukraine and Russia. Those who can capture those food markets can make good money."

Gordie Stanley, born in 1930, grew up on Quadra Island and was part of a large family that loved the sea. All six of the Stanley brothers and their father, Arthur, were seamen—two BC coast pilots, two tugboat skippers, and the rest fishermen. Gordie is a soft-spoken man and he recalls his active life on the sea with fond memories.

I fished until I retired in 1997, trolling, gillnetting and seining. I started fishing on a purse seiner with my uncle, Charlie Peters, when I was about fourteen years old. The first year he paid me a quarter share of the catch but raised it to a half share the next year. He couldn't afford to pay me more so later I started working for someone else. My first command was the *Atalasco* with BC Packers. I had this great big Dane from Nanaimo with me. He was about six-foot-four and the whole galley was no bigger than a table, and oh boy, he had to do some crouching. The first boat I owned was in the late 1960s, a fifty-four-foot purse seiner called the *Miss Toni*, after my daughter. I had that for a few years and then bought a troller, which I used for quite a few years.

On the ocean, things take on names of their own. This 140-kilogram (300-pound) halibut is called a "soaker," and a wall of water as tall as a house is known as a "queer wave."
Byron Wright photo

We often trolled on the west coast of Vancouver Island, off Cape Cook and in Hecate Strait, all of them very rough areas, and I've anchored at Triangle Island north of Cape Scott a few times fishing springs. One time we were fishing halibut near Alaska when what we call a "queer wave" appeared. I was deckhanding at the time and was at the wheel when I saw this wave coming. It was at least as tall as a house and it was just a-roaring. I hollered at the skipper, "What am I supposed to do with this one?" He put it in reverse and we started climbing the wave. When we got to the top where it was cresting, he put it back in gear and the water started coming over us. We couldn't see anything out of the windows. The water was just green until we got through to the other side. We survived and didn't lose anything. Nothing broke. Another boat a couple of miles away from us lost his windows, and his baiting claim [the shelter at the stern where the men baited the hooks] was torn off. We were very fortunate that the skipper knew enough to avoid going into the wave at full speed.

On one trip in the 1960s we left Texada Island and everything was just dead calm until we got to the White Islands. Then we heard on the radio from a fellow who was heading for Steveston that he had run into a bad storm, and he warned everyone to get into shelter if they could. We were already stuck out in the Gulf of Georgia and we just had to keep going. When that hurricane hit, we couldn't even turn around, couldn't do anything, just had to keep going into it. Usually it took us about four hours to get to the Sandheads at the Fraser River. This time it took us all night to get there. Nobody slept.

Once I was running a herring boat, the *Great Northern 5,* for Frances Millard and Company that had the Great Northern Cannery in West Vancouver. We used seine nets for herring with about one-and-a-half-inch mesh. For bigger fish like salmon it's about four-and-a-half-inch mesh. We were in Nanoose Bay on Vancouver Island and

Gordie Stanley: On Triangle Island there's only a cement slab left now way at the top where the lighthouse used to sit. There's a really long and high tramway leading to it. They had to use a donkey engine to raise supplies up to it but how they ever got the donkey in I don't know—there's such a surge. It was quite a feat. When they did get it up, they had to have water for the steam engine.

There were usually thousands and thousands of puffins there. The whole island would be just full. When they took off and flew, it would almost darken the sky there were so many. The last few years that I fished there we would only see a few puffins. They seem to have moved on. The island was full of rabbits, too, probably relatives of those the early lightkeepers brought in for emergency food.

Gordie Stanley aboard the *Great Northern 5.*
Courtesy Gordie Stanley

Gordie Stanley's nephew Rob Stanley with an eighteen-kilogram (forty-pound) spring salmon.

Gordie Stanley photo

had made a set for roe herring that was to go to the Japanese market. In those days the rest of the herring wasn't used. We had Japanese technicians aboard who tested the maturity of the herring. They would tell us if the fish were ready for market—eight, nine or ten percent roe. The Fisheries officer was also on board and he would tell us when we could make our sets, and all the boats had to start at the same time. We were on a quota system and the area was closed to the herring boats as soon as the quota was caught.

Someone asked me, "How much fish can that boat pack?" and I said that we could probably get about sixty tons on it but it wouldn't float. It was an old boat—just a piece of junk. We started loading what we could pack, and meantime this helicopter from the Compensation Board was flying right around us. Our picture appeared in an article in their magazine that came out later. The caption said, "That's what an overloaded herring vessel looks like." It didn't look too good. However, we survived and got into Steveston and unloaded.

We fished up north off the Aleutian Islands for halibut. The closest we got to Russia was off the Pribilof Islands in the Bering Sea. We went into Dutch Harbour where the Japanese planes attacked during the Second World War. We'd stay out on the ocean for days until we needed more bait or other supplies.

Our brother Chuck flew up to Kodiak, Alaska, in 1968 to go out on a fishing boat, the *BC Clipper*. They had just left port and were heading out to sea to fish halibut, and from what I can gather the ammonia pipe for its refrigeration broke and was bleeding right on top of the stove. It started to burn. My brother and two others were down in the fo'c'sle sleeping, and the rest of the guys were up top.

Gordie Stanley skippered the *Great Northern 5*, which was owned by Frances Millard and Co. All herring fished on it went to the Great Northern Cannery in West Vancouver.

City of Richmond Archives, photograph #1999 0006 00785[1]

The ammonia must have turned to mustard gas when it started burning and it seeped down to where the three men were sleeping, killing them. The whole boat burned up. The other men radioed for help and the Coast Guard came out and rescued them from the raft. We figure that the three in the fo'c'sle died before the flames got to them. Chuck was forty-seven years old with three children. His oldest boy, Rick, is now a BC coast pilot.

Rick Stanley, Gordie's nephew, a pilot and tugboater, also tried his hand at fishing.

In the spring of 1980 a partner and I bought a big packer and herring seiner called the *Ocean Aggressor.* On our first trip we went north to Egigik at Bristol Bay on the Bering Sea to buy a load of salmon. We went in off the Diamond D fish cannery because the company I was working for had told me that all I had to do was go in there, load my fish and come out and head back down. To get up to this cannery you have to go up the Egigik River. There was only one buoy up there with a light approximately twenty-two miles offshore, and to go in from the light to enter the river where the headlands are we had to use Loran C because that's all we had for navigation. We'd take one bearing, alter course, take another bearing, and so on until we worked our way into the river.

We got in to the camp, and they said that there was no deal set up with us, and they had to load their own fish first. Once their cannery was full, they wouldn't take any more fish, but the fishermen would still have fish they wanted to get rid of. We could only spend so much money on fish, and the price had gone up that year so we couldn't afford to buy their catches at the price they were asking. So I got the cook to make a big pot of soup, got a big package of popsicles and lots of pop. Then we went around to all of the anchored fishboats and told them to come over and have some pop or soup or make a sandwich. PR work is what I did. I told these fishermen straight out that I couldn't afford to pay the prices being asked. The best I could go was about a nickel a pound less than what they were getting.

All this time we were anchored waiting for the cannery to get loaded up, but there was an eighteen- to twenty-foot tide change and the bottom was hard clay so my anchors wouldn't hold. I was on shore dealing with the management of Diamond D and next thing I know the boat's drifting downriver without me on board. After that we always had to steam slowly ahead on the ebb tide.

When the cannery finally did get loaded, the fishboats started to come over. At one time I had about fifteen boats hanging off me, so I loaded our packer up in one night. She carried about 105 tons of fish. To make this trip we had carried five thousand gallons of fuel, plus we had fifty barrels of fuel on deck, but that still wasn't enough. We had to go in to Dutch Harbour to buy more so we could get home.

We were just about ready to head home when the antenna for our Loran C broke off. Now the only navigation we had was a radar that showed about seven miles, so we had to use dead reckoning. I left Dutch Harbour and followed the Aleutians along up to the coast of Alaska toward Trinity Island. I was worried because the fish had been on board for so long. I knew that I had to get rid of the load, even though it was refrigerated. So from Trinity Island I headed straight across toward the mainland and worked out the course I needed. I didn't have gyro. The magnetic compass had been changed daily for variation so the lines of variation to true north changed as I was going across. So I set the autopilot and allowed for wind set. Four-and-a-half days later, there was Dixon Entrance leading to the Canadian shore. I hadn't known if I was going to see Alaska or the Queen Charlotte Islands (Haida Gwaii). We were lucky.

About a day later we went in to Port Simpson to unload our catch. I identified myself, and the manager of the Port Simpson Cannery said she'd call me when she was ready for us. That was okay but the fish had been on board now for sixteen days, frozen in brine. I waited for a while. A boat came in, unloaded, and went out. So I went up to the dock again but she still didn't want us. We anchored out again. Another boat came in and went out. Another, then another, then another. We're still sitting there. Finally late in the afternoon I went back to the dock and asked if she was going to unload us. She told me in no uncertain terms and foul language that she still was not ready. I went out again. When she finally did call us in, I wouldn't talk to her. I had the engineer deal with her. I found out later that they had been putting all of the BC fish through first, then cleaned out the equipment, then put the Alaska fish through to avoid contamination. I didn't know this while I was waiting. We worked the boat until the next year and then sold it. Too many problems.

Larry Rouse fished for twenty-six years out of Pender Harbour. For part of that time he had his own thirty-six-foot boat, the L-Jay-R. His wife Margaret fished with him for five or six years in all kinds of weather. They live on Texada Island in the Strait of Georgia.

When I was about fifteen, Dad and I had anchored out on our cod boat and a gillnetter came alongside and anchored. Dad went on board the boat to visit the man and his wife. She wanted to make some tea for them all. There were two cans on deck, one holding water, the other gasoline. By mistake she filled the kettle with the gas and put it on their Coleman stove to boil. The kettle caught fire and she grabbed it and threw it out of the back door.

Unfortunately my Dad was standing there and the fire spilled down the front of his body, and she had flames on her hands and arms. They jumped overboard. I got onto the boat and the owner and I had a terrible time getting them out of the water. I could smell burnt flesh. The two of them were shaking, in shock. We wrapped them in blankets and took them to St. Mary's Hospital, which fortunately was just around the corner from Garden Bay. They both needed skin grafts but were later okay. The boat survived as it was just a small fire on board.

At one time I was deckhand on a seiner. We made a set with the seine net, and here was a young black bear caught inside the cork lines. We waited to see if he would swim over them as the net was coming in but he didn't, so the skipper decided to brail him aboard. We dropped him into the fish hold wondering what to do next. He was snarling and snapping but obviously pretty tired by this time and he finally took a death hold on the centre post in the fish hold.

Someone said that we should put straps on him and winch him out. The problem was, who was going to go down into the hold with him? Finally one of the deckhands offered to go and was able to attach a couple of straps around him, but it was difficult. We then hooked the double falls block—like a wooden pulley with two wheels—to the straps. We headed for the beach and lifted the bear out of the hold and lowered him into the water. The poor little guy was all tuckered out by then but he made it ashore.

My boat, the *L-Jay-R*, was a combination troller and cod boat. That meant that we had two watertight bulkheads between the engine room and the stern that we used as live tanks. We'd take plugs out of the bottom of the tanks and seawater would fill them to about a two-foot depth. Then we'd keep live herring or perch bait in one tank and the cod that we caught in the other.

When I would go out trolling with the Missus, we would take our little black dog Bimbo with us. Every morning when we landed the first fish of the day on the boat, she would have to smell it and bite at it, then she ignored the rest of the fish brought aboard during the day. One morning while she was attacking the fish, she got caught by her tail in the V-belt that runs from one gurdy [a spool holding the trolling lines] to the other while they were turning, and they pulled her into the gurdy. She was screaming before I could get the motor turned off.

We didn't have a vet in that area, so we called the hospital and they said that they didn't deal with animals. Her whole back end was badly injured so we had to do something. My wife had a good idea. She called the hospital and made an appointment for Baby Rouse, wrapped the dog up in a blanket like a baby, and we were admitted at the hospital to see a doctor. He looked at the dog and said, "You must think a lot of that dog" and agreed to fix her up. She lived.

I have been involved in some rescues over the years. We were at Skookumchuk Rapids one day and saw people waving from a sailboat. It was obvious that they were in trouble. They had hit a rock and were caught on it by the keel, and the tide was going out. We went alongside and told them to put a line as high up on the mast as they could, then we attached the end of the line to our fishboat. We pulled from the side, the keel tilted and the boat slid off the rock. All part of life on the water.

Don Pepper grew up in Alert Bay and first fished in 1952 on the FV Jean W. Fishing financed his university education at UBC, the University of Surrey (UK) and the University of Wales in Cardiff where he received a PhD in fisheries economics. He served ten years in Ottawa in the Department of Fisheries and Oceans under Romeo Leblanc. Returning to BC in 1980, he taught economics at

Don Pepper in 1959 aboard the old BC Packers salmon seiner the *Northisle* with a catch of unusually large dog (chum) salmon. Fishing financed Don Pepper's academic studies, including a PhD in Fisheries Economics from the University of Wales.
Courtesy Don Pepper

BCIT and was able to fish salmon in the summer, usually aboard the FV Prosperity with Byron Wright. "I have fished summers for twenty-nine years," he says with enthusiasm, and he still continues his summer fishing ventures.

I financed my way through university by fishing. As soon as I went on a fishboat, bang! we started catching. I gained a reputation for being lucky, and at the age of sixteen I made $1,500, enough for tuition at UBC. In a good season I would have lots of money and go back to university. In a bad season I would have to wait, so it took me a number of years to get a degree, which I finally did in 1965.

I didn't pay attention in graduate school at UBC so I got kicked out. I then decided to go to England to university, and for three years I was a transatlantic fisherman. I would fly to England in the fall, attend university, fly back to Vancouver in May, get a job fishing for summer herring and salmon and earn enough money to fly back to England and more university. This was actually cheaper than going to UBC. I'd keep my sea bag with all my fishing gear in various places in Vancouver.

In 1966 I came back to Alert Bay from university in England and met Freddy Jolliffe, who told me that he was one man short for the summer herring and wanted me to come with him. I said okay and put my gear aboard. We had eight crew members and we each got two dollars a ton. That was big money in those days. The boat was an

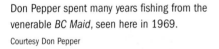

Don Pepper spent many years fishing from the venerable *BC Maid*, seen here in 1969.
Courtesy Don Pepper

old wooden BC Packers boat called the *Vanisle*, a double-decker herring seiner that packed a hundred tons of fish. We were going into the reduction fishery, which meant we would take the herring to the plant at Namu. The *Vanisle* had an old-time system, a Puretic power block, which was a spinning wheel up on the mast to bring the net in, allowing a real reduction in manpower, and we had a herring seine and what we called "the lights" to pit-lamp the fish—which was legal in those days.

Pit-lamping was a rather unusual technique to catch the fish. You would equip your boat on the side with a bunch of mercury vapour lamps or just very strong lights, street lights. Then you would find a good pit-lamping spot, one with a very good bottom where the herring were liable to congregate. You needed a dark night, no

The *Northern Dawn* is ready for pit-lamping, a technique that predated sonar equipment. Pit-lamping required a dark, moonless night so that the light of the mercury vapour lamps could lure the herring—often a hundred tons or more—into an unseen net.
UBC Rare Books and Special Collections, Fishermen Publishing Society 1532 903 1

moonlight. You'd anchor up, shut off the main engine and turn on the lights. They were powered by a small generator. You waited to see how many fish would come to the lights. We didn't have sonar in those days, so we would get the power-skiff man to go around with his sounder and see how many fish were in the set. Anything less than twenty tons you didn't want to set up. If you did it right, you'd have a hundred or more ton of herring brought to the lights.

The trick then was you don't want to turn off the lights, but you've got your anchor down and you have to get it up because you want to catch the herring in the net. So we had a two-skiff system. We had the power-skiff that towed the net, and another skiff called the dead-skiff that had a little Honda generator in it with a couple of little but strong lights like in the big boat. Now we had anxious moments because you could scare them very easily. So you'd switch off the lights on the main boat and, if everything went well, the fish would move from the lights on the big boat to the lights on the dead-skiff. If they did, you then had to get the anchor up and set the net. You started the main engine very quickly because once you did start it, the big noise would scare the fish away, but then usually they would come back to the lights. Now you had to pull the main anchor out very carefully, but one of the most irritating noises for the herring was the sound of the anchor chain in the chock, so you'd just

B C's commercial herring fishery began on a small scale in 1877, when 67.5 tonnes were caught and sold for food; the catch increased steadily into the early twentieth century, especially after 1913 when purse seining for herring became legal. A dry-salted fishery aimed at Asian markets flourished from 1904 to 1935. As this market declined, the use of herring for reduction into fishmeal and oil increased, peaking in 1962–63 when 237,600 tonnes were caught. This fishery ended abruptly in 1967 when the high rate of exploitation and offcoast environmental conditions resulted in a dramatically reduced survival rate for young fish. When the fishery resumed in 1972—mainly to supply herring roe for the Japanese market—it was very closely monitored. Both seiners and gillnetters were now licensed to participate.

The herring industry began as a small food production industry. With the arrival of industrial machinery, however, massive amounts of herring could be fished for fishmeal and oil production. This reduction fishing quickly affected the fishery and it ended abruptly in 1967. By the early 1970s, the herring stocks had begun to recover but the industry is now closely monitored.

City of Richmond Archives, photograph #1985 0004 00510

bring in the anchor to the end of the cable and leave the anchor hanging in the water on the end of the chain, so it would be down about twenty fathoms.

Then you'd cut the dead-skiff loose with its lights still on, and slowly put the clutch in on the main engine so the big boat could creep away from the fish. Any noise would spook them so, while this was going on, you'd never slam a door or drop anything in the engine room. No noise. Once away from the fish, you'd drop the net, get the power-skiff away towing the end of it, and you'd have the herring encircled. The dead-skiff would be still in the middle of the net so the power-skiff had to go and pull him out. When this was all done, it was darker than the inside of a cow, a very touchy-feely situation. The process was so effective that we almost wiped out the herring, and the government closed the fishery for a number of years.

The fishery opened at two on Sunday and closed at two on Friday. We would leave Alert Bay Sunday about noon, run up to the Hope and Nigei isles just off Port Hardy and fish there because the herring would move inshore to feed on the red and green phyto-plankton and zooplankton bloom that came in May and June. We'd find the herring by looking for red feed.

I recall one time on the back side of Nigei Isle the currents pushed all of the feed, which was on the surface, right alongside the island for about a mile and a half, about ten feet wide against the shore. A school of herring would go against the tide and, like a big feeding machine, would go straight along there and take up the feed. Sometimes we would catch them that way, making a little open set as they came along. Once we'd caught about a hundred ton of them, we'd run to Namu to the reduction plant. When we pulled the hatch-boards off, it would look like pink ice cream in the hold. There would be about a foot and a half of pink foam from the red feed. And when you looked at the herring, you'd see that the feed had been so acidic that it had burned the skin right off them. Like nude herring.

At this time the crew was all from Alert Bay, but our cook was a former Newfoundlander called George. He was a figure of fun, of course, because he spoke with a Newfie accent. He also had trouble with his Hs—he'd say, "I put my 'ed in the hoven." He was a terrific cook but he had one signal failure: he could not make hotcakes. He didn't know that you should put the baking powder in last so they wouldn't go flat, and you should have a very warm, not hot, frying pan or stove because if it was too hot the outside of the hotcakes would burn but if not hot enough the insides weren't cooked.

George could not master the hotcake situation. I remember this one time we had a set and got a full load, a hundred ton. This was early in the week so everyone was in a good mood because we'd each already made $200. It took several hours to brail the fish aboard, and George promised us a treat. He would cook us up a good breakfast. Which he did. A good fisherman's breakfast—bacon and eggs, sausages, fried potatoes, toast and, as a treat, he made hotcakes. Again they were just terrible. We didn't say anything, just battened down the hatches and took off.

It took us about eight hours to run from Scarlet Point to Namu. We reached the reduction plant about four in the afternoon. As the union delegate on the boat, my job was to verify the landings. As the herring were moved into the fish plant, I had to check the tally, so I'm up talking to the tallymen about fifty feet above the boat in a very noisy situation. One of the tallymen looked down and said, "What the hell's going on down there?" We could see the cook standing on the boat and the two crew unloaders on the dock pointing to the boat's hull. So the cook peered over the bulwarks at the side of the boat, became visibly agitated, climbed over the bulwarks and got onto the dock. He looked up and down along the boat's hull, then ran along the side grabbing at something. A man possessed. He could see me about a hundred feet away and started shouting and screaming, running around and waving his fists as if he wanted to fight me. Someone had taken all the leftover hotcakes, about ten of them, punched a hole in the middle of each one, attached little strings to them, and hung them along the side of the boat as bumpers. George was infuriated. It was such a funny incident that everybody teased him about it. Unfortunately, he blamed me. It wasn't me, though I must admit that it was the sort of thing I would do.

As we didn't have a pump, we used a brailer to move the fish from the net to the boat. This is a big dip net with a handle and a special little release mechanism built in. You'd have the fish alongside, maybe a hundred ton of herring, and you would attach the brailer to a line, then swing it over the side, and the man on the handle would tilt it up and it would scoop up the fish. The line attached to the brailer moved it forward through the fish on a pulley system called a China haul, which was a little boom, sticking out inside the boat, that the line went through. When you lifted the brailer up, you'd have about two ton of herring in it. Then you'd swing it across over the hatch.

The guy who operated the release was called the asshole man—

unfortunately I don't know any other word for it—and he would trip the little lever and the fish would drop out of the brailer into the hatch. He'd close up the bottom of the brailer and we'd do it all again. A good crew could get a nice rhythm going. As you made your first dip, you'd pull the boat over ten or fifteen degrees, scoop up the fish, the brailer would go across the boat and it would tip the other way, and you would release the fish. The boat would be rocking, port to starboard, port to starboard. A good crew would keep the rhythm going and bring in the fish very quickly.

Currently the herring roe fishery is managed in a pool system with vessel quotas. Each vessel will have two licences to ensure enough wages for the crews; they would have, for example, a 130-ton quota. And they're forced to join a pool of eight other boats that has a pool captain who meets with the Department of Fisheries to determine

There are no normal hours when fishing; fishermen routinely scout all night once an opening has been called. Unfortunately, even long hours aren't always enough to keep a company afloat.
BC Archives, I-29318

when the fishery will open. There are test sets going on all the time to measure the herring roe percentage, which is the amount of roe in the herring. When it gets to 10, 11 or 12 percent, everyone gets anxious because at 13 percent roe content, they'll open the fishery.

You are not allowed to set unless the Fisheries says you may. They may say that we can open at seven a.m., and each pool captain will call in for his boats, and say, for example, "This is the Confisco pool, and our first boat to set will be the *Vanisle*." Each boat will call in before they set, and the pool captain will call in the amount caught by each boat. This allows the Department of Fisheries to have a running tally of what is going on, to monitor for the total limit for the area and avoid overfishing. In a way it's not a very exciting fishery. You know that you're going to get your quota because if some boats get more than their quota they share with the other boats in the pool. You get your fish even though you don't set your net."

Byron Wright has been fishing commercially since 1958 when he was fourteen and he moved with his family to Alert Bay. During the first few summers he crewed on seiners, trawlers and gillnetters as far north as the Bering Sea, and it was this summer income that helped to pay his tuition for two years at Simon Fraser University. In 1967 he decided to devote ten months a year to his fishing and began a mainly profitable career with his own boats. His story illustrates a long and difficult commitment to achievement that eventually resulted in his economic success. His is not a typical fisherman's story.

Byron Wright began fishing commercially when he was fourteen years old. By his mid-twenties he was boss of a skid row beer parlour crew that routinely brought in so many fish they needed to be cargo brailed.
Courtesy Byron Wright

In the fall of 1968, at the age of twenty-three, I talked BC Packers (BCP) into letting me run a boat. They had one that was tied up because it was breaking down all the time. I told them I'd do my best to keep it going if they'd give me a chance. Which they did. I got a crew of four experienced guys out of a skid row beer parlour and gave them an advance, which they invested in cases of whisky. We headed for Alert Bay and fished around there for two weeks. The third week was the last of the season for chum salmon, but there was a southeast wind blowing that made it difficult for most of the boats to work. So we went into an area in Parsons Bay and started to set in front of the reef. The other skippers didn't want to set there for fear they'd blow onto it, but I was a bit more of a risk taker. We would drop the anchor just when we had about three-quarters of the net in. The anchor would grab and the crew would pull the net aboard over the stern or they would brail, then I'd run up and engage the anchor winch and that would pull us out of the rock pile. Then I'd rev the engine up—vroom, vroom—that would tell the guys I wanted to set right away and we'd go back to the beach and set again. At the end of the day we had fish up to the hatch coaming.

When we came into Alert Bay to deliver, I had one of those great moments in my life. The manager, Norm, had been a minister's kid when he moved to Alert Bay and he was kind of resentful of me, just as a matter of policy. He was always making my life a little difficult. When I came in this time, he was in charge of the packer, and I came alongside and spoke to the skipper, kind of pointedly ignoring Norm. I asked the skipper what was the best side of the boat to cargo brail on, which means you've got an awful lot of fish. Now all the other boats had been in there unloading 50 fish, 100, 200, because the weather had blown them out. The skipper couldn't believe that we had enough fish to cargo brail until we opened the hatch covers. He

Byron Wright's vessel, the FV *Prosperity*, with a 326-ton set of herring in Baynes Sound, Strait of Georgia, in 1990.
Courtesy Byron Wright

was amazed and called Norm over. "You've got to see this!" You could have knocked Norm over with a feather. Revenge is sweet when it comes. That was the end of the season and we took the boat back to the company.

The next year they allocated me the *BC Maid,* which was a charming old piece of junk, but once again I worked it night and day and kept it going. I had it for two years. We did relatively well. There weren't lots of fish but we fished where the most valuable were—lots of springs and sockeye. We made 782 sets during the season. But the boat was breaking down all the time.

At the end of the season the manager for BCP at Alert Bay told me we'd ended up number two in all of their boats. So I said, "I guess I'm going to get a new boat next year." He said, "No, we've got a plan for you. We're going to put a lot of money into that boat—a new engine, move the drum on deck, et cetera." I said, "That'll be nice for the guy that runs it. But that's not me. You have thirty-two boats here, any one of which is better than that one. I want one of those other ones. Maybe the guy that was number seventeen or thirty-two should move to the *BC Maid* and I'll move over to his." He said no. As the winter went on, they would discuss it with me because they didn't want to lose me as a skipper. But I wouldn't agree. So as it was getting on for spring, they were getting anxious. That's when I told them that if I was going to run somebody's piece of junk, I wanted my own boat. "You guys have a whole bunch of boats that are sitting in Celtic Shipyards on the Fraser that are condemned or derelict or don't have a current steamship inspection on them. I'd like to buy one of those." I went down and looked them over. There was one, a sixty-foot-long seiner, the *Invercan V,* that was basically a good boat, but it had the drum in a well and an old cat engine, and the boat itself was poorly maintained. I offered them $15,000 for it "as is" and they were to finance it. I had a net and $5,000 as equity but I needed that for repairs. We argued back and forth and I finally purchased if from them for $19,000 and they agreed to put it through steamship inspection.

I took it to Alert Bay before the season opened and started working on it right away, fixing it up. That year a lot of springs and coho had come in early and others hadn't left that area over winter. They'd built up in the bays where they were feeding off the small herring schools. I got my crew together and in June, while everyone else was still working in the net loft, I started fishing. Everywhere we went was fish. We just cleaned them out of the bays. Then we dressed them, which was unusual for a seine boat to do, and sold them to a troll camp and got twice as much as you'd usually get for them. We did very well the first week, and everyone else was getting antsy about how much we were catching. The crew made $700 to $800 a man. The next week we went all the way up to the Nass River around Wales Island and delivered to the camp in Prince Rupert. Then we moved on to Wales Channel and so on.

Come the fall, with the season coming to an end, I didn't want to tie up the boat, so I would go out on weekends with one crew member and jig for cod and ice them. I'd take some salmon and cod plus a few halibut to the dock on Campbell Avenue in Vancouver. Here it was, winter, no one else's fish is coming in and I'm bringing in all this fish that looks gorgeous. There was one Chinese lady, Ruth Sing Lee, and she'd buy everything I produced at good prices.

It was still only November, so I started buying clams from the Indians at Gilford Island. They'd come out on my boat and use it as their work platform. At first I worked as an independent, then I went for Seafood Products. Finally we had produced over a million pounds of clams with that old boat. I'd come to Vancouver with a load of clams so heavy that my insurance company suspended me. We then came up with a scheme. Besides the clams, I would load the boat up with things like scrap iron and brass. Also, the Indians in the villages piled up their beer bottles under their houses, so I took old clam sacks and bought the bottles for a couple of pennies apiece. Each sack held about five dozen bottles. I'd stack them across the boat's stern. So the hatch was loaded with clams, the deck was loaded with scrap and on top was a load of beer bottles.

In town after I got rid of the clams, I would find a load to take back up. For example, the village of Alert Bay needed culverts. I loaded the hatch with vegetables—lovely Marketing Board potatoes for $2.30 a sack—and they went down the hatch with sacks of onions—you'd have to be careful with onions because any moisture would cause them to lose their leaves—and sacks of carrots. The hatch-cover would go on, then I'd put culverts for Alert Bay on top as high as they'd go. On top of that I'd put fibreglass speedboats that people had bought in town and were taking up coast. Then I'd put a bridle on the stern and tow another bigger boat behind me. We'd unload in Alert Bay then go to Port McNeill and sell the vegetables. I'd spend the afternoon phoning around to tell people I'd be at the dock the next morning selling sacks of potatoes at $5 a sack—one

hundred percent profit. They loved it because they would have had to pay $9 or $10 at Shop Right in town. Then Shop Right started buying off me. The volume just went through the roof.

Afterwards I'd go back to the Indians at Gilford Island and they ordered stuff from me like groceries, pop and chips, fishing gear, rain gear and lanterns. I made a deal with them that I would pay them on the last day of the clam digging. Each clam digger had his own book in my galley so the stuff that was billed to him went on the first page and the clams they dug went behind. At the end of the tide I'd tally them all out and give them the cash. When they were digging, I'd come back to the boat early and make one big pot of coffee, like a big stewpot, and another big pot of hot chocolate, and everybody could come back and be out on deck socializing. And when I took them back to Gilford Village, we'd be going down through these little passes with the tape deck going full bore playing Janis Joplin and such. It was kind of fun. The Indians were great to us and we were fair with them.

During that time I ended up financing things like a wedding, a house, sports equipment, prescriptions and other things that people needed in Alert Bay. At the end of it all only one guy shafted me and he had planned to do it right from the start. He told me that he needed money for a prescription for his grandmother, but he bought booze.

During that winter I'd made enough money to buy a new radar. I hadn't had that basic electronics aid before. And after the spring clam season I hired two guys to help me sand the boat right down. We painted it and called it *Prosperity*. At the end of the winter I had enough money to put a new drum up on deck and install a nice new stern platform.

Later we went north and stumbled into some fish in a place called Kitasu Bay. It's the most amazing place. It's just full of sealife—crabs, clams, whales, porpoises, basking sharks. We found a way to fish there without putting too much pressure on the gear. In any bay that faces away from the outside ocean, the fish get blown in but they have to get back to the ocean, so on their way out they follow the beach rather than being scattered all over. There were southeast winds blowing the fish in, but I was sheltered in the bay so I could fish. We had the boat just about loaded with sockeye and spring salmon. Just amazing. The company finally assigned us our own packer. We had a tremendous season. We came home and took about two-and-a-half loads of chums out of Qualicum.

Byron Wright began his successful fishing career out of Alert Bay. When his ice hatch was free of fish, Wright loaded it with fresh vegetables and sold them on the Port McNeill wharf for half the price being asked by local vendors. Soon, even the Shop Right was buying potatoes and onions from him.
BC Archives, I-21958

I wanted to upgrade my boat because people were starting to fish herring again and I couldn't. Just to fish herring you had to be born into it. It was very difficult to get jobs. I ended up buying the *San Juan I* in 1972 from a guy that was famous for being tough to deal with. We went to the Admiral pub and did a deal on a paper napkin for $112,000. He tried to get out of it the next morning but I wouldn't back down. When I got the boat from him in the middle of winter, he had stripped everything off it—all the fuel, the oil—every-

thing he could strip. He left me one broken-down crescent wrench.

I had a plan to make the boat better. How herring boats sink is that the load of fish can blow the bulkheads out when they flow back and fill the stern. So I bought a whole bunch of square steel stock and aluminum penboard and other materials. In Alert Bay I found that the government had decided that the lumber on the dock was too old and they were putting down new boards. People in town were shaking their heads because the ones coming off were better than the

Byron Wright bought the *San Juan I* in 1972 for $112,000. The deal was signed on a napkin in the Admiral Pub on Hastings Street in Burnaby.

City of Richmond Archives, photograph #1999 00060 1875[1]

ones going down. They were beautiful fir. I made a deal with the shipyard that they would take them off, sand and plane them, and I'd pay for the blades because there were a lot of rocks ingrained in some of these boards that would screw up their machines. When they finished, I had a pile of beautiful fir planking. I got a local guy to come down and I hired a crew of eight to ten guys to work with

At a herring opening in Barkley Sound, the crew of the *Snow Prince* sets up the drain for the herring pump.

Brian Gauvin photo

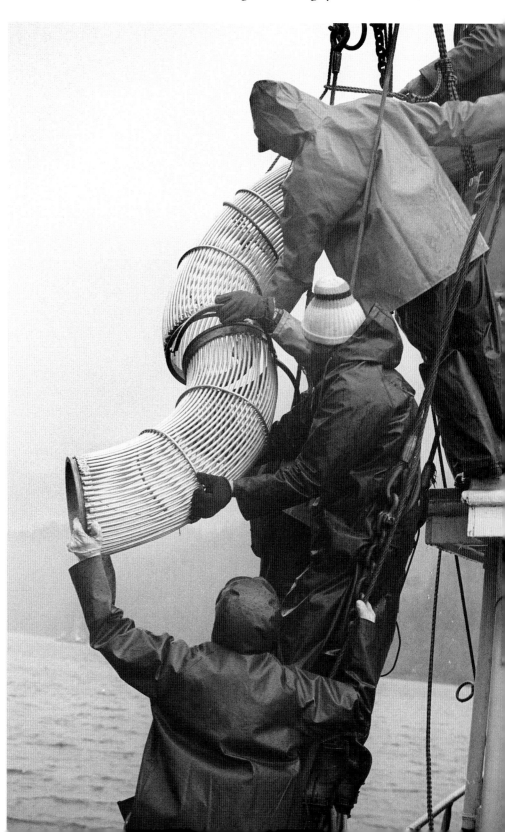

him. We did the bulkheads in steel and put steel stanchions in for the penboards, all in steel, and some of this big planking. It was solid.

The company decided that all their boats were going to fish in one pool. Eleven other guys and I bought sonars, something new for us. It was a good move. But all of the boats were going down to Tofino and having a big meeting so I knew something was going on but I didn't know what. Turns out they wanted the company to take me out of the pool because I hadn't fished herring before. In those days you could start to fish when you wanted, so we went out to Sydney Inlet at night and were cruising around when the sonar showed a big blob under the water. I put my seine out and the whole school swam into it.

We weren't very experienced with herring so we drummed until we pursed the rings up, and then I phoned the *Canadian No. 1,* a BCP boat, to ask for assistance. He came alongside me and when he saw how much fish I had he called in a big packer, the *Hesquit.* They helped us dry up, that is, pull the rest of the net in, which we didn't know much about, but we were watching very carefully because we had to learn. We pumped fish over to the packer until it was full, then put the rest of the set into the *Canadian No. 1,* altogether about 240 tons, our first set. Then we made another set close to the beach. By this time it was coming daylight, and I could see that there was now no fish anywhere around, so I went in to the bay at the closest anchorage, dropped the hook and went to sleep. The radio was next to my ear and I heard someone talking about the *San Juan I.* One of the skippers came on and said, "Look at that lazy bastard on the *San Juan I.* He's in there anchored and the rest of us are out here scouting around." Then someone else came on and told him about our catch that night and said he thought I was deserving of a little nap. There was a big silence over the air. That was the end of them trying to get me out of the pool.

We stayed for two more days loading other boats in the pool, and then the boss told me to take a load myself and head for town. Now I was very tired. I'd been going for days on adrenalin. As we were coming across the Gulf of Georgia, I could see the lightship and everything was clear except for a little fog further up the Gulf. I told the crew to keep going the way we were but to give me a call in two hours. However, our old radar wasn't working. In about two-and-a-half hours I heard them slow the engine down. I had just jumped out of my bunk, when Boom! Boom! Boom! the boat bounced up on the rocks at the Fraser River jetty. We were in a really, really bad

The *Seaspan Valiant* is familiar with early morning rescue calls.

Courtesy Seaspan International Ltd.

situation. We couldn't back off and we were in heavy fog. We were locked there. It was dead high water and we were loaded. If the tide went down with us like that, it would break the boat's back.

I phoned Air-Sea Search and Rescue immediately, requesting a tow from someone with lots of power. The tug *Seaspan Valiant* came along—twelve hundred horsepower—and I told the skipper that I was going to put bridles all over our boat. I attached them to the bottom of the mast, went around the hatch coaming, through the bulwarks, from the drum stand—all over the boat. I put a big strap on and then took the tug's towline and connected it to my strap. I told him to let out as much line as he could, up to a thousand feet, then turn so that when he hit the towline he would be directly opposite me and towing at full throttle. Our new sonar had a big heavy tube underneath, and it had literally locked behind a rock, so we had to lift the boat off.

The tug began to pull, and at the same time I had the power-skiff going and the boat was going full in reverse. The crew stood behind the cabin so if the line broke nobody would get killed. As it slid off, the noise from scraping the rocks was horrendous. Afterwards we headed up to the BCP Imperial plant unloading docks at Steveston. I got in right away and unloaded the fish, then went to the shipyard and left that night all repaired and with a new radar installed. All of our careful installation of heavy boards and metal supports in the hold had certainly paid off, and we went on to a good first season.

In 1973 the Department of Fisheries decided to limit entry to salmon to protect the resource, so there would be no more A licences granted. Now a licence could only be granted to replace another licence and they increased the price and the requirements. Previously you could go out and pay ten dollars for one, so immediately they became kind of a black market commodity. These were the first licences to be severely limited.

In the meantime I had decided I wanted to build a new boat because the *San Juan I* was very limited—poor fuel capacity, old equipment, big clumsy old boat. I liked the look of the new aluminum boats. They were performing very well. The marine architect said that the new boat would need forty tons of A licence, so I had to go and buy that tonnage from other A licence holders. I went to BC Packers and they said they would help, but the price would be $400 to $600 a ton. I told them okay, just get the licences as quickly as possible because I thought the price was going to go up. The following week they still hadn't bought any licences for me. By this time the prices were up to $800 to $900 a ton. The next week they were up to $1,200 and I decided to quit fishing until I acquired licences. I took an ad in the paper that said, "Will pay up to $2,500 a ton."

I got a flood of responses. Several of these guys just wanted to keep their boats but not fish commercially for salmon any more. I had just moved to Vancouver and got a lawyer, and we drafted three different types of agreement, which meant that we were basically buying options. I acquired enough licences for my boat and still had a whole stack of responses. No one else was following up on this idea, so I was the only game in town if a guy wanted to sell. So I bought some more. Then I saw some nice little boats being built, 15 and 16 tons, so I acquired licences for two of them. I acquired a lot of options and the price kept going up to $3,500 a ton. BC Packers agreed to buy my extra options for about $250,000, which mostly paid for my new boat before we even started construction. At that time I was the right guy in the right place doing the right thing.

We built the three boats in 1975. The aluminum *Prosperity* did very well. I took the best of the technology that everyone else had and brought it all together in that one boat. It became very efficient. During the next 15 years we were a top-producing boat in the industry. I put in an RSW System to chill my fish. They would come

With the inevitable loss of income, fishermen's strikes, like this one in April 1981, proved difficult to wait out in the face of the massive loans needed to buy more efficient boats, expensive licences and the necessary tons of salt used as fish preservative.

Dan Scott, The Vancouver Sun

aboard my boat up my stern ramp and go below into refrigerated seawater, chilling down to optimum temperature, which is just above freezing, 32.5 °F, because you don't want to freeze the eggs. The fish would come out of the hatch just beautiful. I delivered fish to the plant in Steveston and they were literally still jumping as they went along the conveyor. I told the manager that we should be getting more for these fish than those guys over there delivering garbage out of a hatch where they didn't even have ice. Their fish looked like rags they were so long in transit. When the company said no, I set up my own processing company. We called it the Quality Fish Company, bought a piece of property in Delta and set up offices on Broadway in Vancouver. We netted millions of dollars in the first season. It was very successful. Then we decided to build a new plant in Vancouver for herring processing and we operated it for seven years.

Then a terrible catastrophe occurred. There was a fisherman's strike. The Japanese had advanced us $4 million for herring and we had already spent money on tons of salt, advanced money to lease licences, hired people and carried out capital improvements. We'd incurred all of these expenses and with no season forthcoming we immediately lost about $4 million. There was no way to get it back. We fought for four years to try to stay afloat. In the meantime I had bailed out a lot of young guys who couldn't make their boat payments so I ended up on the hook for their indebtedness, too. I'd had some financial reserves going into this but they got chewed up pretty quickly over the four years. I then had problems with my bank.

I bought a new colour sonar for the boat, but while they were installing it, one of the guys drilled through its cable, and the next day I found out that they were going to open the herring fishery that evening. I was in a terrible dilemma. We had someone bring in another cable and we installed it as we were running for the grounds, but we got there just as they closed the fishery. I was not in a very good mood. The next day when they opened it again in the shallows, I was very aggressive. I found some herring in the shallows in among the speed boats and their anchors. I had a plane working for the company and the pilot told me that he could make out patches of dark in the water that looked like fish. So I went in and set. One of our packers came in and we filled him with 135 tons.

Then we got a set near Powell River for 90 tons. We scouted all night to find fish and found that they were coming up to the pulp mill there and then turning back to get away from the noise of all the

The process of moving fish from the ocean to a
boat using a large dip net is called brailing. It
requires plenty of teamwork and a good rhythm
if the fish are to be brought in quickly.
BC Archives, I-29309

boats with their engines running. I was scanning on the radio and
heard one of the Fisheries guys saying, "Here they come again." So I
turned around and ran down there. Just across the line I could see the
schools of herring on our new sonar. So I set my net. We set around
many other boats and they smacked into each other, busted their gear
and swamped their skiffs trying to get out of my net. All the time I'm
coming around blowing that big whistle, then I went slow to let them
get out. We got 300 tons. The next day we caught another 55 tons.
So we got 525 tons in the Gulf. Fortunately, we had a fleet of packers
to bring the fish to town. However, even with all the fish we caught
our product wasn't enough to keep the company afloat.

The Quality Fish Company finally folded in 1984. I left but was still a guarantor, so it carried on for a few months before it locked down, and I went fishing as an independent on the *Prosperity*. We worked very hard. I did the marketing myself. Suddenly I started getting some real money for myself. I was able to pay off the bank. Guys told me that they thought I was down and out. I said, "Hey, don't count me out yet. For so long I've tried to please everyone— my employees, my partners, the Japanese, the banks—and ended up not pleasing anyone. And I particularly didn't please myself. This time around I'm making it a priority to please myself so don't get in my way." I became very aggressive. We worked even harder than before. We did very well.

I sold the aluminum *Prosperity* in 1990 for a million-and-a-quarter, and the guy that bought it has been a top producer with it, too. In 1989 I had built a new *Prosperity*. My objective was to increase its efficiency in every way. In the first season we loaded it up with sockeye and had a bang-up herring season. The boat did so well. I've just now sold it.

Once the net of a purse seiner has been closed and drawn to the side of the boat, a pump is lowered into it and the fish are transported to the seiner's holds or to those of another seiner or a packer. Often, a catch will fill more than one boat.
Vance Hannah photo

There've been some great moments. I had a couple of million-dollar days. One day in Barkley Sound we had 525 tons of herring in the net. It took two days to pump the fish out of it. My other boat netted 160 tons. I sold them all at the average price of over $3,000 a ton. I made over $2 million that day. Another time on the Gulf there was a picture of me on TV with a huge set and the *Eastward Ho* behind me. I filled it and the *Prosperity* and put fish into another big

boat. That was a million dollar set. All the fish were in one wad, and there were only about six of us that got good sets. It was very competitive. As we were setting, the guy next to me pulled a trick. We all usually set to the right, but he made a point of setting to the left so he could cut me off. But I was able to bang his boat as he was setting. On TV they said, "The fishery opened this afternoon at 3:30 in Baynes Sound. Watch this action."

This herring set in Barkley Sound is typical of the congestion that happens once an opening has been called. As dozens of boats try to set their nets on a single body of fish, they frequently collide or run over each other's nets, and though common courtesy dictates that nets be set to the right, competitive neighbours have been known to set to the left.

Brian Gauvin photo

CHAPTER TWO

Rescue and Enforcement

Fisheries and Coast Guard

"We came in with the sea behind us just off Kains Island, right up on top of one of those big waves and surfing. The *Tanu* is a big steel ship, 180 feet, and I'll bet we were going twenty-five knots where usually we go twelve. At double our speed, it was a terrible feeling because we couldn't do anything. We had two engines on her but there was a broken line on one of them so we could only use one engine. I got us down but the next wave came from behind halfway up the mast and curled right over the ship. The whole ship was under water right up to the wheelhouse windows. I couldn't do a thing. Water went right down the stack into the engine room. The engineer phoned: 'What are you doing up there?' Fortunately, everything kept going. She was a good ship."

Captain Ozzie Nilssen

The Canadian Coast Guard vessel *Penac* practises a high-speed beach landing.

Canadian Coast Guard, Pacific Region, Roy Klohn photo

Hovercraft divers are assisted back into a Coast Guard Auxiliary vessel after a training exercise sent them deep beneath the surface.

Courtesy Canadian Coast Guard, Pacific Region

The Canadian Coast Guard was officially created on January 26, 1962, taking over the Department of Transport's fleet of 241 ships and being assigned responsibility for enforcement of Canada's laws and all rescue efforts within our waters. Thirty-three years later, on April 1, 1995, the force was integrated into the Department of Fisheries and Oceans patrol fleet with all vessels, now painted the distinctive Coast Guard red and white, responsible for both fisheries enforcement and search and rescue. The Pacific Region of the Coast Guard is headquartered in Vancouver and Victoria and is responsible for 560,000 square km of ocean and more than 27,000 km of BC and Yukon coastline. A staff of more than one thousand maintains and operates the region's shore stations and a fleet that consists of ships, cutters, helicopters, airplanes, and hovercraft. They conduct search and rescue missions, service lighthouses and navigational aids, monitor fishing vessels, seasonal openings and conservation measures, and support ocean and research sciences.

Captain Brian Wootton, the officer-in-charge of the Coast Guard's forty-five-member Sea Island Base in Richmond, points out that "not all Coast Guard duties are heroic ones. We actually fulfill an important role in keeping the economy moving. It sounds like a strange thing to say but it's totally true, whether it's sending Canadian grain or lumber products in ships around the world or getting new Toyota sedans off a ship that has just arrived from Japan. Along their way those ships will pass hundreds of marine traffic lights and navigational aids, indicating safe passages. How is the Coast Guard involved in this? Ships pay different rates of insurance around the planet to cover the risks to their operations, and Canada is a preferred nation. Maritime underwriters give these shipping companies good insurance rates for plying Canadian waters because we maintain a first-class traffic system, from watching with coastal radar and responding to pollution incidents to sending out assistance when somebody is sick on a ship. Low rates and good infrastructure make it easy for these guys to do business here rather than in many other places, especially where the geopolitics are unstable and problems like piracy still rule the waves—and yes, there are such places even today."

Canada is known internationally for its marine traffic system and it is the Canadian Coast Guard that maintains this vital infrastructure. Light stations and navigational beacons are operated by solar power or diesel generators and require regular maintenance.
Courtesy Canadian Coast Guard, Pacific Region

When winter ice threatens northern shipping routes, Canadian Coast Guard ice-breaking vessels keep the shipping lanes open for as long as possible. The icebreaker *CCGS Sir Wilfrid Laurier* is one of the favoured vessels for patrolling icy waters here in the Dolphin and Union Strait between mainland Nunavut and Victoria Island.

Courtesy Canadian Coast Guard, Pacific Region

"You can think of one of our jobs as a new take on that old joke about it taking five public servants to change a light bulb, but that is what one of our craft is doing right now with a crew of six or seven—they're out changing some fancy light bulbs on a range site. But if we don't keep the ranges going, the bigger ships could get into very expensive trouble. We set up lights, a low one and a high one, and the pilot's job on the ship's bridge is to keep the two lights in line so the ship doesn't run aground. In this way the Coast Guard is the glue that links all the things that make up our maritime safety system: from washing bird poop off the solar panels that keep a critical navigation light burning and guiding ships to where the deep water runs to making sure that channels get dredged, breaking ice and escorting commercial traffic when the heavy ice of the Arctic has brought deep-sea

shipping to heel. It's not glamorous but it's the kind of work that's going on from Newfoundland to the Northwest Territories to right here at Sea Island. It's important work, the lack of which would cause all sorts of safety problems connected with life at sea, and with them many contrary economic implications.

"And all this says nothing about the value of asserting Canada's sovereignty. We have to think of the great white north and of keeping that coast open and recognized as ours by the international community. We send Coast Guard missions to the Arctic every year. The *Sir Wilfred Laurier*, based out of Victoria, is in the western Arctic right now. She is doing resupply and scientific work and providing ice escort for commercial shipping. Icebreakers from Quebec City and St. John's, Newfoundland, are in the eastern Arctic as well. Actually

The Canadian Coast Guard helicopter *Helo* is an ice observer that flies above an icebreaker and directs it along the path of least resistance. These sophisticated helicopters are able to gauge the age and thickness of ice, and the pilots then relay this information to the ship's captain.

Courtesy Canadian Coast Guard, Pacific Region

A Canadian Coast Guard Sikorsky S61-N helicopter takes off on a routine maintenance mission to automated light stations around Vancouver Island.

Courtesy Canadian Coast Guard, Pacific Region

The Pacific Region branch of the Canadian Coast Guard is responsible for resupplying lighthouse keepers with everything from groceries to fresh water. The four square water tanks seen here on the *Siyay* are being pumped into a large reservoir at this light station in the Strait of Georgia.

Courtesy Canadian Coast Guard, Pacific Region

having a physical presence in the high Arctic is going to become even more important to our assertion of sovereignty in the coming years, particularly as global warming continues to melt polar ice, giving freer access to foreign ships in that part of our country.

"Another important job we do across Canada is supplying materials to automated and manned lighthouses. The automated ones are serviced mostly by our helicopter fleet, and if the telemetry—or lack thereof—tells us that there are electrical glitches, we fly technicians out to do the repairs. Some lighthouses, particularly on the west coast of BC, are still manned, so they require physical support—everything from new linens and groceries to water and fuel for their generators so the lights will keep burning. Sea Island Station crews are preparing for a replenishment mission today. They'll be loading thousands of

gallons of fresh water to take up to Merry and Entrance islands, neither of which gets the amount of rainwater we do in the Lower Mainland. Our buoy tenders sometimes carry a helicopter aboard, which vastly increases their reach and their dash-speed to remote work sites.

"The *Laurier* is such a ship; at 272 feet long and with a crew of twenty-six aboard, she's our biggest vessel in BC waters. Of similar class, but slightly smaller is the *Bartlett* at 187 feet long and with a crew of twenty-four. What all these Coast Guard crews have in common is that they may be helping a scientific mission today while tomorrow they're on tanker duty, and at any given hour they may be called upon as search and rescue (SAR) specialists or firefighters or paramedics, only to return to the business of scrubbing the bird crap and painting the buoys when these things are all done. From interesting to boring to adrenaline-pumping and back again, it is what Coast Guard multi-tasking is all about.

"SAR calls at Sea Island average nearly one a day, and we respond using one of our two hovercraft. The *Penac*, which is Coast Salish for fair winds, at eighty feet long and forty-five thousand kilos all-up-weight, is the smaller of our two vessels and is fitted primarily for SAR duty only. The *Siyay*, Coast Salish for friend, is ninety-four feet long and over seventy thousand kilos all-up-weight. She is a very versatile cargo-carrying craft that is better suited to heavy weather than her little sister."

Captain Ozzie Nilssen was just seventeen when he went to sea on a Norwegian tall ship, and for the next nine-and-a-half years he worked on board various freighters, almost never living on land. He came to Canada in 1966 and spent the next thirty-six years working the BC coast on the patrol vessels of the Department of Fisheries and Oceans, serving as skipper on the Tanu from 1978 until he retired in 2002. Although he hasn't lived in his home country for many years, his Norwegian accent remains.

After I came to BC, I started work with the Department of Fisheries and Oceans on one of their smaller boats, the ninety-eight-foot-long *Hunter Point*. Our job was to keep track of domestic fishermen, making sure that they were fishing in the legal areas, though in those days there wasn't much illegal activity going on. If we did discover something, we reported it to the fishery officer at the office—or sometimes there was one on board with us.

Captain Ozzie Nilssen, a Coast Guard skipper, leans on the depth sounder on the bridge of the *Tanu*.

Courtesy Captain Ozzie Nilssen

Two years later I joined the *Tanu* as bosun with Captain Reg McLellan. It was brand new, 180 feet long, one of the bigger offshore boats. At that time there were a lot of Russians fishing off the coast, sometimes up to a hundred factory vessels and smaller side draggers. The offshore limit then was only twelve miles, so they could fish just beyond it. They used to fish along the Charlottes—they would lay a long line of baited hooks along the bottom and fish for black cod— and then go south to lower Vancouver Island to fish hake. If we caught them inside the twelve-mile limit they would be arrested, have to go to court and be fined. In fact, the first boat we arrested wasn't Russian but was a Japanese longliner, the *Kotoshiro Maru*, fishing inside the limit off Hippa Island on the west coast of the Charlottes in 1969. We boarded them and spent the night on board taking the boat in to Prince Rupert where the captain was fined about $10,000.

A former Department of Fisheries and Oceans vessel, the fifty-five metre (one hundred-eighty-foot) *Tanu* became part of the Canadian Coast Guard fleet in 1995.

Courtesy Captain Ozzie Nilssen

Captain Harold Monks: On the *Tanu* we spent a lot of time around the west coast of the Queen Charlotte Islands and Queen Charlotte Sound. In the winter it was an area of continual awful weather. Our foredeck was coated with a composition about three-quarters of an inch thick, a sort of concrete, and on more than one occasion, after bucking into a big sou'easter in that area, we would find chunks of it had been torn off and had landed on top of the wheelhouse.

We also arrested a big Japanese stern dragger inside the closing line in Queen Charlotte Sound. It was the *Koya Maru No. 2* with Captain Ito. A Canadian naval ship had notified us that he was in the area and helped us apprehend him. It was a dirty night with a southeast storm so we took them into Cape Scott where they got boarded and escorted to Victoria. If I remember right, it cost the company and the captain about $70,000. Later on Captain Ito and I became very good friends and he even came to BC on holidays. After the twelve-mile limit was extended to two hundred miles in January 1977, all the foreign vessels had to have licences and we had to go out and issue them. At the same time we carried out entry boarding as well as checking them at certain intervals to see that they were catching the right fish.

In March 1969 we were sent up to the Bering Sea for the first time with the *Tanu* to enforce the halibut regulations and act as a rescue boat because the Canadians were fishing halibut there. At that time the *Tanu* was a very rolling ship, very uncomfortable, and on one occasion we had been out to the Pribilof Islands and were on our way in to Dutch Harbour in a gale when all of a sudden there was a freak wave and the *Tanu* laid herself over on her side, over 80 degrees. The wheelhouse window went into the water and the port lifeboat was in the water. Everyone thought, "Oh-oh!" It was not a nice feeling at all. It's a wonder someone wasn't hurt. The quartermaster was standing by the wheel and ended up underneath the side window. The gyro slewed since it went way past the range of the gimbals. The cook had a full pot of soup on the stove and this spilled on the deck. There was a butter dish sitting on the table and it shot up and stuck on the bulkhead. We had her rolling problem fixed later by putting in new bilge keels and this reduced the rolling by eighty percent, but that didn't happen until 1981 and all that time we were rolling our guts out.

That same year the Coast Guard ordered the *Tanu* to proceed to a ship that had run aground on Ferrer Point on Nootka Island. It was a huge Greek freighter, just sitting there with the bow on the beach. It had come from Japan and was heading for Fuca Straits but had run smack into Nootka Island instead. A little tugboat from Tahsis had put a line on it for salvage and since it was a nice day we went up to Zeballos and tied up there overnight. However, during the night a big storm came up and when we came out the next morning it was blowing hard and we couldn't find the ship. When we got close to the shore, we could see a little bit of the bow and some pieces of the hull up on the beach but the rest had totally been chewed up and had disappeared overnight. Fortunately, all of the crew had been taken off. Even today you can still see part of the bow lying on that beach.

We did a lot of work on our local fishing fleet over the years. We had to board them to make sure that they had licences and that they were legal. For instance, if they were catching halibut, they had to have a halibut licence. The coastal waters are divided up into many areas and the fishermen can only catch fish in the open areas, those that the Fisheries have declared open. We also had big salmon openings on the west coast of Vancouver Island, the Gulf and Juan de Fuca Strait where we opened and closed the areas and enforced the boundaries. We then boarded or hailed the boats to see how much they had caught and we would send the report to the various fisheries offices.

Herring was a high-money fishery—cutthroat and fast and furious. One day the season would be open on the west coast and then a few days later up at the Charlottes and the boats would charge up to the next location. The gillnetters towed a punt behind them that they actually shook the herring into with the aid of a mechanical shaker. There was so much money to be made in herring that if they were fishing off Comox, for example, they would rent a helicopter to pick up the punt and drop it off in Barkley Sound where they had another fishboat waiting to start when that opening was called. Boats were always trying to get ahead of each other. The first few years after the herring fishery resumed in 1972, overloaded boats were sinking everywhere. One year especially was really bad. I think seventeen herring boats sank. The seine boats would travel with the skiffs pulled up on deck and the net on the drum and this would affect their stability. They'd be out in the middle somewhere and be caught in a storm and tip over or sink. Some of the packers were overloaded. There were so many people lost from sinking, it was terrible.

In the early 1980s we were up in Nootka Sound for a herring opening that turned into the shortest fishing opening on record. On board we had a Fisheries officer from Tahsis who had never done a herring opening before, as well as a herring coordinator and scientist and a guy from Ottawa who had just come out to have a look at this. We'd been out there looking for herring for some days, and the seine boats that were waiting to set their nets were getting antsy.

Then one day we got a frantic call from the fishboats that there was a good-sized herring school off Nootka Light and they wanted us to come over and check it out right away. We had to sound out the school to see the amount and also have the test boat make a set so we could see if the herring were mature and had enough roe to make them worth catching, so the Fisheries officer told the fishboats to get off the herring school so we could sound. The fishermen wanted to know if we'd call them in good time and the officer assured them that they'd be called in plenty of time to start fishing. So they moved off and we started sounding.

The test boat made a set and it was decided that the fish were good. Now the young Fisheries officer goes over to the radio and broadcasts, "The area is now open." The fishermen just went crazy because he hadn't called them as promised and they weren't in position to set their nets, and the herring coordinator could not believe his ears and stood there with his mouth open unable to speak. So I yelled to the Fisheries officer, "Tell them it's not open! Tell them it's not open!" So the young officer yelled into the radio, "No, it's not open! It's not open!" Lucky for us there was not one boat ready to set. It was the shortest herring opening we had ever had. The Fisheries officer was so embarrassed he couldn't talk for about ten minutes after that. The guy from Ottawa didn't know what was going on. He kept standing there saying, "What? What?" Of course, after it all settled down, we had a planned opening and all went fine.

In November 1984 we had a fishery up in Kyuquot Sound on the west coast of Vancouver Island, a one-day chum salmon fishery for both seiners and gillnetters. A couple of days beforehand, two boats started out from Esperanza to Kyuquot to take part in it with only a sounder between them for navigation since both their radars were broken. It wasn't that bad of an evening so they thought they would be able to see the buoys and just come on in. They were talking to each other on the radio and finally one of them said, "What's that light ahead? It's not supposed to be there. Oh-oh, we must be in the wrong place."

They had actually gone past the entrance to the sound and ended up at Spring Island. There's a whole bunch of big reefs up there so we called them and said that we would come up and get them and for them not to move. We headed out. As soon as they saw our lights, they started to come toward us, but there was a reef between us so we again asked them to hang on. But after we got out a ways, a lightning storm came up—a terrific wind with huge waves and terrible lightning. The second mate and I were looking out the window and we'd get this sudden terrible flash and all we'd see after was the wheelhouse windows superimposed on our eyeballs while the thunder was shaking the ship. It was just like a welding flash. After a half-hour or so the storm disappeared, but by that time our eyes were itchy and sore—like they had gravel in them—and our faces were actually sunburned. We were finally able to get to the fishboats and guide them safely in to Kyuquot.

A couple of days later, just as that one-day fishery was closing, there was a call for a gale warning but nothing big so as soon as the fishboats had delivered their fish to the packers they started to head home, some of them heading south and others heading north. We waited around and collected all the delivery slips from the packers before going into Tahsis to deliver the tally sheets to the Fisheries officer, but there were so many seine vessels pulled into Tahsis that there was no room for us to tie up so we went on to Zeballos instead.

About one o'clock in the morning we got a call that there were two small gillnetters in trouble up in Quatsino, so we started up the engines and headed out of Esperanza Inlet. When we got on the outside, the wind picked up. We could hear the guys from the gill-netters on the radio talking to the Coast Guard station. The sea was not so bad but the wind was and—because they didn't know the area—we wanted to give them advice to get them into shore in Brooks Bay and into Klaskish. The odd part of this area is that when it's blowing a southeast storm, the wind blows over the Brooks Peninsula and drops down the other side, so the closer you get to shore the worse it is. I guess they got scared and were trying to make Winter Harbour for safety instead.

We got up there about nine o'clock in the morning. The Coast Guard cutter *Ready* was ahead of us but it had to seek refuge in Klaskish Inlet after being nearly swamped. They had asked some Polish factory vessels to help in the search, but every one had some problem or excuse why they couldn't assist. A Norwegian freighter came on the scene but asked to be released due to heavy rolling. By that time an Aurora airplane had arrived and the pilot said that they had seen an overturned boat ahead of us with people on it and that they'd dropped two life rafts near the boat. We found the gillnetter *Silver Triton* just off Lawn Point, but we were afraid that if we got too close we would get caught in the fishing nets they had let out to try to save the boat. They had those blown-up floats attached—what they call scotchmen—and that's what the plane crew thought were

The *Cape Sutil* is a fourteen-metre (forty-seven-foot) lifeboat designed specifically with the self-righting capabilities that prove so invaluable in heavy weather.

Courtesy Canadian Coast Guard, Pacific Region

people. There was nobody there and the boat was upside down. Then the weather got really bad. Meanwhile, the plane had found the other boat, *Miss Robin*, upright but there were no people aboard, so we just hung around there waiting to see what we should do. The wind was so strong that the six-man life rafts the plane had dropped were being rolled across the water like tumbleweeds. One of them got blown right into Winter Harbour.

The plane's pilot then reported that he had spotted two persons in the water and they were waving. He gave us the position and we proceeded toward it, but by now the seas were over forty feet high—huge, the worst I've ever seen—and the wind was blowing over eighty miles per hour. From where I was standing on the bridge of the *Tanu* it was twenty-four feet up to eye level from the sea. The big seas coming at us were so high we weren't able to see their tops through the windows. It's hard to turn around in that kind of sea. When you're bringing the ship around and you get on top of a big wave like that, the ship falls down sideways into a deep hole and then straightens up real quick at the bottom.

Then just as we got to where the pilot had said the survivors were, he spotted what he thought was another person close to shore near Cape Parkins and decided to drop a marker buoy there, so he didn't come back to spot for us for a long time. Now the rain was coming down so hard that it looked like a snowstorm coming straight sideways and we could hardly see across the water, and I was so afraid that when we were coming down off one of those huge waves the people in the water would be right ahead of us. How we would get them aboard if we did spot them I didn't know.

It got dark and the plane had to leave because they couldn't see any more and neither could we. We decided that we would spend the night in Quatsino Sound and go back the next day. We came in with the sea behind us just off Kains Island, right up on top of one of those big waves and surfing. The *Tanu* is a big steel ship—180 feet—and I'll bet we were going twenty-five knots where usually we go twelve. At double our speed, it was a terrible feeling because we couldn't do anything. We had two engines on her but there was a broken line on one of them so we could only use one engine. I got us down but the next wave came from behind halfway up the mast and curled right over the ship. The whole ship was under water right up to the wheel-house windows, and I couldn't do a thing. Water went down inside the vents in the stack and into the engine room. The engineer phoned to ask, "What are you doing?" Fortunately, everything kept going. She was a good ship.

When they'd heard that the plane had spotted another survivor off Cape Parkins, a group of fishermen had left Winter Harbour aboard the seiner *Caamano Sound,* landed a shore party near Hunt Island and walked across to the cape to see if they could see something. Just as we got into Quatsino Sound they called us; they were

Behind every search and rescue mission is a highly skilled team that logs hundreds of hours in training every year. Here, the hovercraft *Siyay* runs through a rescue scenario with an air-sea rescue helicopter from the 442 squadron.

Courtesy Canadian Coast Guard, Pacific Region

trying to get back to their boat but their skiff had tipped over. We had to go back out to rescue them. They were just behind Hunt Island in Forward Inlet and we managed to get them to their boat by using our inflatable rubber boat. On the way back to Quatsino Sound we spotted the hull of the *Silver Triton* close to the beach east of Montgomery Point. By this time it was nine o'clock at night and I had spent that whole day from one o'clock in the morning on the bridge. I couldn't leave the throttle so crewmembers had brought me sandwiches.

The next day we went out and continued the search. It was now just blowing forty so the crew thought it was a nice day. We found parts of the *Silver Triton* totally smashed up on the shore near Montgomery Point. The engine was attached to part of the hull, and underneath the engine was the body of a person in a survival suit, jammed in there with his head out one side and his legs out the other. He must have been inside the overturned hull when we came alongside the day before, but of course we had no way of knowing. The helicopter found two more bodies, the crew of the *Miss Robin,* on the shore at Lippy Point later that morning. We also found a survival suit from the *Silver Triton* drifting ashore. It was a very emotional time.

One year in the 1980s there was a big body of sockeye off Sand Heads at the Fraser River's mouth so Fisheries decided to have a seine fishing opening there, and the *Tanu* was called in as a management platform. Being so close to the river mouth, this was a high-profile fishery, and we had so many Fisheries officers and managers on the boat plus about five media people with their big cameras that I could hardly get into the wheelhouse. Some of the officers on board had never been involved with managing a large fishery opening before, though it was old hat to us because we had done it so many times.

The opening was announced on a special frequency that the fishermen could listen to but couldn't talk on. The officer in charge tested the radio to be sure he could be heard and then announced, "The next time you hear a voice on this frequency it will be the opening." So everyone was waiting. Meanwhile, one of the small Fisheries boats called in on another frequency to ask the guy standing by the radio to do another test. So I said to the guy, "No, don't do that! Don't do that!" The guy didn't listen to me and went on the radio saying, "This is the *Tanu,* one, two, three, one, two, three." And, of course, this was the next message from the *Tanu* and the fishboats started to set their nets. The Fisheries boats out on the water began calling in to report that they had caught fishermen setting and they took their names and made them haul their nets back in. It finally got straightened out and a proper opening was carried out. Fortunately, the media guys didn't catch on, so it didn't come over TV or it would have been embarrassing for the Fisheries. There were lots of red faces that day.

Another time, in 1983, we were west of the Finger Bank off the lower west coast of Vancouver Island on our way out to check on tuna when we saw something on the radar. It was kind of a misty afternoon and we couldn't see anything by eye so we thought we would head toward it to check it out and see what was there, but all of a sudden it disappeared. Then after a while it came up behind us. So we turned around and headed that way. We did that two or three times and each time it would disappear and reappear behind us before it finally disappeared. Two days later on a clear night we were about two hundred miles offshore and there was a submarine sitting on the surface with its amber lights on. I guess it was his periscope we had seen on the radar and he had been playing cat and mouse with us. I don't know if it was a US or a Russian sub.

In the early 1990s we were on patrol at our southern border with the USA outside Fuca Straits, checking the border for shrimp draggers and black cod fishermen, when we saw a big Russian spy ship, the size of a small cruise liner, sitting south of the border, just outside the twelve-mile limit. We could always recognize them by their big white domes on top of the ship. There is a telephone cable that goes out in that position and they were sitting right on top of it, probably listening. There was also an American navy ship hanging around there, but he took off, and I thought that we should go closer and have a look at the spy ship. Suddenly when we were about five miles away he blacked out both our radars. There was nothing on the screens. The Russians were probably laughing and saying, "Look what we can do to you." The radars came back after about fifteen minutes and we went slowly around him and took pictures. They had a big camera on the bridge that followed us around. But nobody could do anything about him because he was outside the legal twelve-mile limit.

When the Coast Guard and Fisheries were merged in 1995, we became Coast Guard, our boats were painted red and white, and after a few years we did mostly search and rescue. Foreign ships didn't come inside as much as they had, and Fisheries had observers on

In 1995 the Canadian Coast Guard was
integrated into the Department of Fisheries and
Oceans and became responsible for both
fisheries enforcement and search and rescue
operations. Rescue training, like this exercise at
Wreck Beach in Vancouver, is an on-going
endeavour.

Courtesy Canadian Coast Guard, Pacific Region

many of the domestic boats so we didn't have to check for illegal
catches anymore. There's also someone on the dock now checking
quotas while the boats are unloading. That's not to say they couldn't
go in somewhere else and that's also not to say that there wasn't any
poaching going on. By that time many of our crews and officers had
been trained in enforcement at the RCMP Academy in Regina and
at the Justice Institute in New Westminster, and we became full-
fledged and armed Fisheries officers with the same powers as those
ashore.

On August 10, 1999, we got orders to go to the west coast of the
Queen Charlotte Islands to see if we could find a migrant ship
reported heading into that area. There were a lot of fishboats around
but no migrant ship so we proceeded into Skidegate Channel to wait
for the RCMP, Canada Customs and an emergency response team.
They joined us there late at night and told us that the migrant ship
was running erratically back and forth offshore west of the

Charlottes, shadowed by an Aurora aircraft. It was after midnight when word came in that the ship was heading into Cape St. James so we set out with the *Arrow Post*, which is a Fisheries patrol boat, and the RCMP catamaran *Inkst*er. We sent the RCMP vessel ahead because it was faster, but they didn't get there in time. Several of the RCMP guys got seasick; their commander was up on the bridge trying to talk on the phone and he had a bucket right beside him. The migrant ship, which turned out to be Korean, had already dumped all of its Chinese passengers off, and the aircraft pilot reported she was heading out again. We went in near Barber Point north of Cape St. James and we could see a whole beach-full of people.

In August 1999 the apprehension of a "migrant ship" carrying illegal Chinese immigrants to the BC coast was a "multi-agency" operation involving the Coast Guard, Citizenship and Immigration Canada and the RCMP with standby assistance from the Canadian military, the Rescue Coordination Centre and Parks Canada. The crew aboard the RCMP catamaran *Inkster* included trained assault boat operators, a dive team, an emergency response team, two police service dog teams and an interpreter. On August 11, while the Coast Guard and Immigration people attended to the 132 migrants abandoned on the extreme southern end of the Queen Charlottes, the *Inkster* set off in sustained eleven-foot seas to intercept the fleeing ship, finally stopping and boarding it thirty-four miles offshore in international waters. The ship and its crew of nine were escorted back to the Queen Charlottes and later to Vancouver. Two days later an RCMP emergency response team returned to the area to search for missing migrants; all but one were retrieved.

In August 1999, the Canadian Coast Guard was alerted that a Korean ship carrying illegal migrants was nearing the Queen Charlotte Islands. Capture of the *Hueg Ryong* was a "multi-agency" operation involving the Coast Guard, Citizenship and Immigration Canada and the RCMP, seen here aboard the illegal vessel. Courtesy Captain Ozzie Nilssen

As soon as we found out that the Korean ship had dumped them off it became a search and rescue operation, and the *Tanu* was appointed on-scene commander. It took us five hours to get them off the beach using rubber boats going back and forth to the ships. We took over seventy on the *Tanu* so we rigged a tarp for a roof on the afterdeck and put them there. The *Arrow Post* did the same and they took about fifty. We also managed to catch the Korean ship, the *Hueg Ryong*. It appeared that they got scared when the Aurora aircraft flew low overhead and turned back. The RCMP went on board and nabbed them. Later there was a court case but, because the Koreans said that they had been hijacked and the court couldn't prove that they hadn't been, they were let go.

Some of the migrant people tried to get away. One man got wet and when brought aboard he was very hypothermic, close to dying. The Corporate Health Service had two doctors and of course we had our own medics, and they worked on the man on deck. He was pretty well gone and almost died twice. Luckily we had a reheating unit that

By the time Canadian Coast Guard officials had been informed about the migrant ship the *Hueg Ryong*, it had already dropped its passengers north of Cape St. James on the southern tip of the Queen Charlotte Islands. It took the crew of the *Tanu* five hours to ferry the migrants from the shore to the boat.

Courtesy Captain Ozzie Nilssen

generates steam. It had been on board for quite a while but that was the first time we had ever used it. Luckily the guy came around, but we had to helicopter him out to Queen Charlotte City. The saddest part was that a sixteen-year-old boy took off into the bush when he saw us coming and we never did find him, so there's a body up in the bush somewhere on Kunghit Island.

Going down the coast to Port Hardy, we had a total of 104 people on the *Tanu*. We couldn't feed the migrants very much because they hadn't eaten much in their two months on the ship. We learned from a previous group of migrants that had come into Gold River not to give them too much to eat at first because they would be sick. So we gave them broth, rice and water. It was quite interesting to have planes and helicopters dropping supplies of blankets, rice and water to us by parachute.

When we got down to Port Hardy a crew came aboard to process these people, and they all wore haz-mat [hazardous materials] suits—big white suits—and goggles so you couldn't see what they actually

Once aboard the *Tanu*, the migrants were wrapped in blankets and housed under a large tarp on the ship's stern. As they had not eaten much for the two months they had been aboard the *Hueg Ryong*, they were given simple meals of rice and broth so that their systems would not be shocked by rich food.

Courtesy Captain Ozzie Nilssen

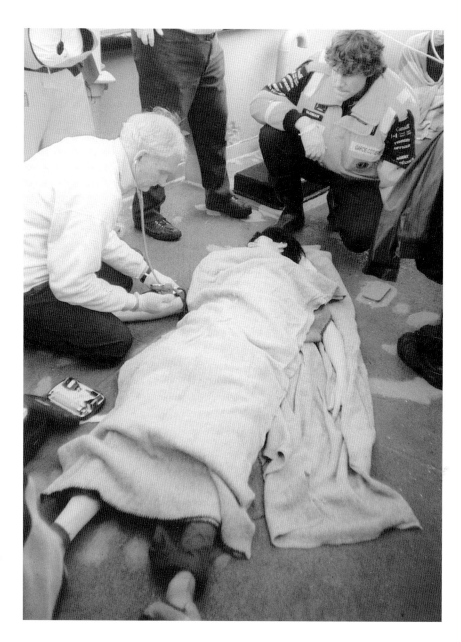

A Corporate Health Service doctor attempts to revive a hypothermic illegal Korean migrant aboard the *Tanu*.

Courtesy Captain Ozzie Nilssen

looked like. We had been looking after the migrants wearing our regular clothes and we thought, "Is there some health issue we should be concerned about?" So after the migrants left we had to disinfect the whole ship because we didn't know what kind of sickness they might have brought aboard. The Immigration people separated those they thought were the snakeheads, the people smugglers, from the rest. They got searched pretty well, marked with tags, and their hands were tied behind their backs when they went ashore.

We were so lucky with the weather. In two more days we wouldn't have gotten them off that beach. They would have been ashore there for a week because a southeast came up. Biggest darn rescue I was ever involved with.

Captain Harold Monks, a former BC coast pilot, also served with the Department of Fisheries for a few years in the early 1970s.

I worked for the Department of Fisheries the summer of 1974 on their largest vessel, the *Tanu*, and that was when I had what I would probably call my greatest disappointment at sea. At that time there were Japanese and a couple of Korean longliners fishing black cod off our coast, and Russians, Poles and other Japanese trawlers were fishing hake and ocean perch. The *Tanu* did offshore patrol work and was very well equipped, and we were patrolling along the closure line for foreign fishing vessels between Cape St. James at the southern end of the Charlottes and Triangle Island at the north end of Vancouver

When the *Tanu* arrived in Port Hardy, a crew of immigration officers wearing hazardous material suits boarded the boat and began to process the migrants.

Courtesy Captain Ozzie Nilssen

Island. It was hard to determine where the line was in that area because when you were just a few miles along it you lost sight of land both visually and by radar. We had to use Loran and an echo sounder to navigate—these were the days before GPS—and to get a fix or position, two bearings were required to create a cross on the chart.

We very seldom caught a foreign fishing vessel inside as their navigation systems were very good and if the foreign fleet know you're around they don't dare try. But it was good publicity for the Fisheries whenever they caught some vessel inside. This particular time there was a Korean longliner about halfway down from Cape St. James with his gear out, and we suspected that he was inside the boundary. In addition to the Loran and sounder we took several sun sights with the sextant and then went away and double-checked the sextant calculations. The only thing that didn't seem to jibe was the soundings. One set of Loran lines in that area was very unreliable but the other Loran readings plus the sun sights indicated that the Korean was definitely well inside the line. I contacted the Vancouver office and after considerable deliberation they called back on the radio phone and said we couldn't make an arrest on the strength of the Loran as it wouldn't stand up in court. Those in the office didn't understand the significance of the sextant sights, the sun positions, which were very accurate, more so than the one set of reliable Loran lines we were using. We were told to board him and simply give them a friendly warning. This we did and he picked up his gear and never returned. It turned out it was his first venture along our coast.

We went back the following day, sounded the whole area, and took sun sights along with Loran readings every fifteen minutes. There was a gully in there about four hundred fathoms deep that wasn't marked on the chart. The Korean had been just going by the soundings, and he was about four miles inside the line, but his sounder indicated that he was outside. We sent the results of our survey with all positions and soundings to the Hydrographic Department. They went back to their original surveys and found that there actually was a gully there that for some reason had never been included on the chart. A "Notice to Mariners" came out shortly afterwards, indicating the chart error. So this experience was my greatest disappointment: we couldn't arrest him.

Captain Brian Wootton has always had an interest in the sea, influenced by family stories of the navy and merchant marine and by going with his father, a customs officer, to clear deep-sea ships. He started fishing summers as a deckhand when he was seventeen years old, saving his money for university, but after studying for two years at UBC he enrolled at the Coast Guard College in Sydney, Nova Scotia, the only college of its kind in Canada. While there he met his future wife, Cheryl, who was also in Coast Guard training. After the three-year program he returned to Vancouver where he took up duties as navigation officer at the Sea Island Base in Richmond. He is now the officer-in-charge of that station and very proud of the services the Coast Guard provides across the country.

Captain Brian Wootton, Officer in Charge of the Sea Island Coast Guard station, has always been fascinated by the sea.
Courtesy Captain Brian Wootton

When I first started here I was full of piss 'n' vinegar. I loved this. I thought it was all about the need for speed. That was my own focus. I have to admit I loved the movie clichéd "dark and stormy night" call. They were the adventures I loved the most. Now I'm at the stage in my career where I like the calm water on the other side of the gale. I've turned into a sucker for the happy endings, and I don't want to see the news helicopter hovering outside the station gates when the shift is done.

The incidents that really galvanized my love of these vessels and the work that this station does occurred on a dark and not so stormy night when I was first assigned to the West Coast. It was a night thick with fog, the kind we often get in the early fall, and the air ambulances were grounded because of the total lack of visibility. A brave family had lost their son in a car accident in Nanaimo, and his body was being sustained by machines because they wanted to donate his organs to anyone in need. The call for a medical transport found its way to my crew. A surgical team of seven was sped to Sea Island from where we transported them to Vancouver Island in the fog. They worked their magic there and we brought them and their precious cargo back to Vancouver just before dawn. The doctors all seemed to be very tired but excited as they explained that several patients were in operating rooms at various Lower Mainland hospitals waiting for their arrival. The next day we found out that somebody had received a heart and lungs, someone else had received a life-saving liver, two people had been saved with new kidneys, and someone had had his sight restored. As I said, this was early in my career, and I couldn't get over it. I had basically just done my part as a taxi driver, but without our radar guidance skills, that ride, those rescues, would not have happened.

About six months after that we had a big incident involving a lost person in the waters of Boundary Passage. It seemed like the whole

At the start of his career Brian Wootton loved the adrenalin rush of being called out on a "dark and stormy night." Today he prefers the calm water on the other side of the gale.

Courtesy Canadian Coast Guard, Pacific Region

world had been searching for him. He'd been out on a dive charter and become lost upon surfacing in the current. There were three or four Canadian Coast Guard ships out looking for him, US and Canadian Coast Guard helicopters, and 442 Air Force Squadron resources. We had just arrived on night shift and were requested to gear up and head south for Boundary Pass to join the other hover-craft, crewed by the day shift, because she would be running out of fuel at some point soon and would have to leave the search. I was a neophyte at search planning at that stage and was relieved that there was already an on-scene commander down there so that I could simply focus on my own set of search instructions from him or her.

When we got down to a place called Tumbo Island I reported in to the on-scene commander and said that we were available for tasking. He was overworked because of all the resources he was trying to coordinate and told me to stand by. So while we waited I did my own small search plan, drawing out some boundaries for the search on my electronic chart. I told the hovercraft pilot and the lookout to start steering for a red flashing light right ahead on a particular course. It was well dark by this time, but both crew kept reporting to me that there was no such light. All they could see was a flashing white light against the dark horizon. I told them to stay on that course while I checked my charts and coastal pilot notes again, trying to pinpoint a white flashing light on that bearing. I thought I must have missed something or that I had an old chart that had not been updated. Still we stood on.

As it turned out, in spite of the roiling current, this missing young fellow who had been swept away from his dive charter boat had had the presence of mind to climb out onto a buoy. He was exhausted but he smashed out the red lens on the buoy light and managed to get inside the cage where he tied himself to the structure. So at that point all that was broadcasting from this buoy were the five lonely white light bulbs inside what should have been a coloured lantern. This, of course, meant that all we could see was the flashing white light. We steamed on our original course until we got to the flashing light, and the lookout started screaming, "He's there! He's there! He's in my light!" In the meantime the on-scene commander had finally radioed to detail my tasking, setting out courses and boundaries for us to search. It was all I could do not to interrupt him and tell him that he could send all his resources home, that we had the survivor and would transfer him to Sidney for medical examination but that "he looks good." That eureka moment with its feeling of euphoria is as good and glamorous as it gets.

Another time we got a call from the Area Control Centre [air traffic control] that they had heard from a helicopter in distress and wanted us to go and find it. The pilot was fully equipped with VHF-AM radio but that was all. All he knew was that he was over top of a Coast Guard beacon, but the fog was too thick to carry on to Vancouver and he could not turn around and go back to Vancouver Island for the same reason—he was not equipped for instrument flying. So we

jumped in our craft and headed out. Based on his description of the beacon, we hoped he was off Sandheads because there are a lot of lights out there for ships entering the river. We started dialling with our fancy direction-finding equipment and did manage to receive a very weak signal from this guy. We homed our way to his position and got out to what we call the "hooter buoy," which is properly called the Roberts Bank Beacon. The fog was so thick that we had to slow down to almost nothing, totally at the mercy of our radar.

When we arrived at the beacon, we could see the landing skids of the helicopter above us but not the rest of it. The pilot told us that he could see the strobe light on our tail section. We asked how he was fixed for fuel, and he had only ten minutes remaining. We were just over eight nautical miles from the airport and we could do a maximum speed of fifty-five knots. By my reckoning the trip would take nine minutes if we could do it at flank speed, something not recommended given the lack of any visibility. We told him to use our strobe light as a reference and to follow us. We couldn't see him at all in that configuration and had to rely on our radio link to make sure he was still with us. So we got the hammer down and started speeding back to Sea Island, only to have—for the first time in my career and still the only time all these years later—an aircraft ask us to please slow down. He was getting disoriented trying to keep an eye on us and on his altitude at the same time. We slowed down with the clock still ticking.

As we approached the airport, I called the tower and told them we had the helicopter under escort. We were about two miles off our base in the middle arm of the Fraser when like magic we burst out of this big wall of fog and into beautiful daylight. It was wonderful. We looked up and watched the helicopter as he began to accelerate away. He got straight on the radio and thanked us, and then called the tower to ask for permission to fly over to the north side of the airport instead of the south side, another minute of flight time. The tower sombrely informed him that permission to divert to the north landing pads was denied. There was already a Transportation Safety Board (TSB) investigator waiting for him at the south side landing pads. It turned out that the passengers on that flight were the producer and star from the *MacGyver* television series. They'd been over in Victoria filming and they had been desperate to get back to Vancouver where there was shooting going on, too. They had twisted this pilot's arm into making the trip even though he knew that fog

Navigational buoys are meant to steer ships away from dangerous waters and they are closely monitored to make sure their flashing lights are always working. On more than one occasion the Canadian Coast Guard has found nearly drowned victims clinging to their cages.

Courtesy Canadian Coast Guard, Pacific Region

The hovercraft *Siyay* comes home to rest at the Sea Island Coast Guard station after an arduous search and rescue mission.

Courtesy Canadian Coast Guard, Pacific Region

had been reported. The TSB takes this kind of thing very seriously, hence the speedy arrival of investigators to talk to the pilot. Later the production company and pilot showed up in person to thank us for our help.

Another one of my favourites happened in Boundary Bay. It is, in fact, a typical coastal story of poor planning and bad luck, sprinkled with a large measure of good fortune. Two fellows had gone out in a car-topper to catch some crab for a family barbecue and were overcome by an unexpected westerly gale, one that turned the swells into surf off White Rock. Their boat rolled over and one guy, who was a strong swimmer, managed to get ashore. When he looked back out onto the bay, he couldn't see the other guy, and we were tasked on a search for him along with a US Coast Guard helicopter.

We found our man. He was on top of the international boundary marker a couple of miles from where he had spilled into the water. The current had swept him away from the beach to the base of this beacon and, though it was a falling tide, he was just able to reach the bottom rung of the old steel ladder leading up the base of the beacon. He had hauled himself out and climbed the sixty feet or so to the top of this tower, and the weather had then started to deteriorate mercilessly. He was now suffering from serious hypothermia. The wind was blowing at more than thirty knots and he was fully exposed to it in soaking wet clothing. Our first choice was to direct the US helicopter to the beacon, hoping they might hoist him from his perch. However, with darkness falling and the wind too strong to manoeuvre the hoisting basket to the tower, the helicopter could not safely do the job.

We realized that one of us would have to keep piloting our hovercraft in the weather, leaving only two of us to try and get the fellow down from above. Fortunately, one of our crew was a bit of a mountaineer, so he went up the tower and I went with him. When we got to the top of the ladder, we found that our survivor's legs were immobile and looked like wax, but he was still conscious and happy to see us. We rigged some long-line gear with a jury-rig girdle of sorts to go around this poor guy because his limbs just weren't working anymore, and then our mountaineering rescue specialist managed to belay us from the top of the beacon as I man-handled our new friend down the ladder. I was holding this guy up against my body with one arm wrapped firmly around him and my other partially around him while I tried to keep a few fingers gripping a rung. We must have looked rather comical in our giant bear hug. Together we lowered him down close to the craft, and the captain did a fantastic job in horrendous weather to hold the hovercraft at the base of the beacon. The most exciting part was trying to time our jump to the craft, because it was rising and falling on the sea. The crewman above had to give the rope slack at the precise moment that the hovercraft rose on the waves and I kicked away from the beacon to land on what looked like a ridiculously small landing area in front of the pilot's windscreen. But it worked like a charm. We smacked onto the outer deck and rolled into the main cabin. It was a good

The *Penac* hovercraft is a medium-sized vehicle that floats on a cushion of air called an apron. It is capable of working in very shallow areas and can travel at speeds of up to sixty knots, making it the ideal vessel for search and rescue or environmental incidents where response time is critical.

Courtesy Canadian Coast Guard, Pacific Region

search, a first-class rescue, good teamwork with the other resources out there, and there was the omnipresent dose of good fortune with his buddy surviving to make it ashore and raise the alarm in the first place.

Bad luck's got a lot to do with the typical call of this kind, but bad planning's probably the other eighty percent of the problem. Everything from the first trip of the year in the boat to "What do you mean the cellphone's not good enough?" This is actually a fairly common problem in recent years—people abandoning their VHF marine radios in favour of their cellular phones. For searchers, though, the problem is that you cannot pinpoint a cellular phone signal without an extraordinary amount of technology, both hardware and software, so most rescuers cannot direction-find your signal to see where you are when you call on a cell. If you have an old-fashioned or new marine radio, we can find you because the Coast Guard has direction-finding equipment up and down the coast. Bowen Island has a big transceiver, Mayne Island also, and Helmcken on Vancouver Island. There are primary stations in Comox and Prince Rupert and peripheral sites as well. We have put antennas on mountaintops along the coast to make sure we can maintain the VHF coverage in as many remote places as possible.

Tim MacFarlane always had an insatiable appetite to serve and decided to pursue a career in anti-terrorism or air-sea search and rescue. He joined the Coast Guard in 1990 and after graduation from the Academy moved to BC. A muscular man, he has always been a very strong swimmer, and he hoped to be able to jump from helicopters into the sea to rescue people, but when he saw his first hovercraft he knew that was for him. After using his own scuba gear to aid in rescues, he eventually helped create a Coast Guard dive team. His years in the Coast Guard have been better than he hoped for.

A Coast Guard officer since 1990, Tim MacFarlane was instrumental in creating a Coast Guard dive team.
Courtesy Tim MacFarlane

In December 1997 our crew was awakened in the middle of the night at the Sea Island Station to an emergency locating transmitter (ELT). It sends a signal to the SAR satellite that then sends a signal to a Rescue Coordination Centre, which tasks the local asset, Coast Guard or military. Our hovercraft has some elaborate directional finding equipment, so we got on board and were soon doing forty or fifty knots getting out into the Strait of Georgia. It was a beautiful, crisp, cold, flat calm evening. The visibility was about ten kilometres. As rescue specialist, my position was in the front left where I could operate what is called the "night sun," a sixty-million-candlepower searchlight, and I could control a certain part of the radio package so that if the radio traffic got too intense for the navigator she could pass some of it off to me during the search. So I was the lookout for the team and searched for any targets in the water.

As we got into the area where the ELT was going off, out of the corner of my eye I caught sight of what looked like a sheet of typing paper floating on the surface of the water. I got the gut feeling that something had to be up because paper doesn't float terribly long. I looked over at our pilot, Tim Theilmann, and he looked at me. We both had a weird feeling about it. Sue Pickerel, our navigator, was in the back seat directing. We saw more paper and bits of debris, so we knew something had happened. We quickly found out that a large fishboat, the *Pacific Charmer*, had sunk.

I spotted a life raft in my night sun searchlight and tons of debris everywhere. Tim brought me right up to the raft, which had a canopy on it, and I jumped on board. I had the sensation that it was sinking and then we realized that it was still attached to the vessel. I hopped back on board our hovercraft while we decided what to do. We thought maybe we should dive on the boat so we contacted the Rescue Coordination Centre at Esquimalt base and asked them to send every available asset. We stood there searching and talking, and I

Many victims are unable to swim to a rescue boat once it arrives on the scene and must be rescued manually. Hovercraft crews log many, many hours practising how to rescue fatigued, hypothermic and injured victims from the water.
Courtesy Canadian Coast Guard, Pacific Region

was using what is called a "night fighter," a smaller night sight with a golden glow instead of a piercing white light. I scanned to the right of the machine [the hovercraft] and saw what looked like a cloud of steam or vapour. Then, as I looked more closely, I could just make out a jawline and a pair of glasses. It was a guy in the debris field clutching what looked to be a log. What I'd seen was his breath. We turned toward him, Captain Theilmann hopped out of the pilot's seat and the two of us went to the front of the machine while First Officer Pickerel moved it toward the person in the water. The captain leaped out of the machine, grabbed the survivor in the water and, as he did, I grabbed the captain around his legs. Because the machine—with its momentum—could not be slowed down quickly enough, we ran over the survivor. It was only for four or five feet but enough that they were pushed underwater under the machine's skirt. However, the captain hung onto him long enough for me to pull the two of them out from underneath.

We pulled the survivor to the front and I opened the ramp, which is a door you can lay onto the water to pull out survivors, and Tim and I pulled this guy out. He turned out to be as big as the doorway—at least six feet tall, three hundred pounds. He had been in the water by now for over an hour with no life jacket and he was extremely hypothermic. I tried to lift him into the machine, but it turned out to be more of a coaching job on how to crawl. He crawled from the front of the machine into the back, where I began my medical protocols—taking off the wet clothing, wrapping him up, getting him heat pads, talking to him. Of course, with a survivor in that situation, you want to get as much info as you can as quickly as possible. He might have been the only person on board, which would mean that we could shut this down and take him to the hospital. I remember asking him how many people had been on board, and it went everywhere from twelve to twenty. At some points he couldn't even talk but he finally told me, "There were five of us. I could hear them all screaming just before you guys got here."

As I was doing this Tim and Sue were turning the machine around. The survivor we got next was the DFO observer. He was the one clutching the ELT. He knew enough to grab that thing and not let go. His wife had bought him the flotation jacket that he had on. When they started motoring toward him, Tim and Sue yelled at me to get up front because they had a survivor. So I left the guy I was working with, making sure he was semi-stable, ran to the front and got ready to receive this other guy. All he was mumbling was "Don't let the crabs get me!" Given another half-hour in the water he would have been toast. No doubt in my mind. He was completely, severely hypothermic, poor motor skills, mumbling and no more shivering. That was past. Those are definite signs of severe hypothermia. I brought him to the back and tried to keep him talking to me but he wasn't coherent. I also had to keep monitoring the first guy.

I'm not sure if it was a helicopter or someone else who had spotted the next individual. He was just in jeans and a T-shirt and had swum for the bluffs. Now he was standing on the top of a rock at the base of a huge cliff and there was no way up, out of or around this thing. We went and plucked this guy off. He was hilarious. He had your typical east coast, not-a-big-deal attitude. That's just the way life is. A great verbal orchestra coming out of him, which was great. I actually instructed him to help me with the two other guys.

The *Pacific Charmer*, a large steel-hulled fishboat, was licensed to pack but not to fish herring, yet it had been entered into the Department of Fisheries lottery to fish food herring in the winter of 1997. At 1:15 a.m. on December 2 there were five men aboard as the boat dragged nets in Pylades Channel just behind Valdes Island. The crew had eighty tonnes of herring aboard and were making a last set. Their plan was to load another nine or ten tonnes, anchor for the night and make the twenty-mile journey to Vancouver in daylight. At 1:29 a.m. the net was being hauled up the stern ramp when the *Pacific Charmer* listed to port. It paused then, as the net was hauled higher, rolled to starboard and didn't come back. Water poured through the manholes that were open to receive the fish as well as through other starboard openings. It down-flooded the after part of the hold through a door into the engine room that had been tied open because of the calm weather. There was no time to launch the life raft before the boat went down.

While we were doing this, they yelled that they had found a fourth guy, but he was lying face down in the water. We didn't know how long he'd been face down, so I had to act as if it had just happened. We pulled him into the machine, and he's what we call foaming. It's like someone takes a Gillette foamy can, puts it inside your throat and presses ON. It just comes spewing out. It's non-stop foaming. This happens when water mixes with the lungs. It creates this sort of cocktail, like Alka Seltzer. I kept wiping the fizz off his face, tried to suction a bit of it and did CPR. I was doing this in the alleyway between the pilot and navigator who were trying to run the machine, but Captain Theilmann was also trying to hold the body down for me because it was hard to get him in the right position. The whole time I'm doing this I'm just a curtain away from the three survivors. Remember, these guys were buddies, so I don't want to send these severely hypothermic guys into a worse state of shock, knowing that their crewmate is getting CPR.

By that time another Coast Guard vessel had come into the mix. Tim contacted them and asked if they had a rescue specialist on board because now I had four casualties. I was getting a little taxed and knew that I needed an extra pair of hands, but I was having a good time. Jeff, the rescue spec on the other Coast Guard vessel, came on board and began helping me with CPR. Then he went in the back to see the other three guys. He'd brought a "heat treat" with him that supplies heated, humidified oxygen that re-warms the patient from the inside out. I had one already going.

We got to shore at Ladysmith Harbour and were going to drive right up the ramp, because the hovercrafts can do that, but there were logs washed up all over the ramp, and the people in the ambulance didn't know enough to come down to the machine. They just stood there waiting because they hadn't heard that I was doing CPR on someone. They only knew that we'd found three hypothermic people. You can imagine their surprise when I leaped out of the machine with buddy over my shoulders, doing the fireman run uphill to the ambulance. There were two young EMTs on it but we needed two people for CPR so Captain Theilmann told me to leave with them. One assisted me and the other drove. We whisked off to the hospital, code three, lights, sirens. I was doing compressions while the EMT took care of the airway. We didn't know how long our patient had been underwater and hoped we still had time to save him. We got to the hospital so fast that the on-call doctor hadn't even arrived yet. When we went to get the paddles on our patient it became confusing

because the unit wasn't powered up and the nurse couldn't understand why the machine wouldn't turn on until someone figured out
that it wasn't plugged into the wall. We were all working on him but
at one point he lost his bowels, which is usually a sign that you're
done. I left him in good hands, raced back in the ambulance to the
machine, and out we went again to look for buddy number five. By
now it was coming on dawn, everything a bluish tint. I call it the
"nasty misty blues" because so many of the bad calls come at that
time of the day.

     We heard from two guys in a fishboat who thought they'd seen a
survivor clinging to a log. We whisked over there as fast as we could.
It turned out to be the skipper. His head was high and dry out of the
water and he was clutching a log, but his body was stiff as a board.
Sue helped me bring his body on board and the smell made it
obvious that he had lost his bowels. We bagged him.

     On the way back I couldn't help but think that we'd gone the

In a Rigid Hull Inflatable Boat (RHIB), a
Canadian Coast Guard skipper responds to the
early morning grounding of a sailboat. To Coast
Guards, dawn is known as "the nasty, misty
blues" because so many emergency calls come
in at that time of the day.
Courtesy Canadian Coast Guard, Pacific Region

Captain Brian Wootton: "At one point we used trained divers in the Arctic to help with ship repairs and such, but they were gradually dropped from that service and came south and joined our station crews. In some cases they ended up where they were the only diver among a crew, and they would go out on our SAR calls and carry their own scuba tanks and regulators. But there's lots of risk attached to diving with a team, to say nothing of going it alone. Because we're one of Canada's busiest search and rescue stations, throughout the nineties this station launched a pilot program to deliver a modest program safely. It was successful but not without lots of road bumps and headaches and lots of concern in the rest of the Coast Guard about sending our people into danger.

When the diving service was withdrawn it attracted a lot of attention here, and now we're the only station in Canada that's been given permission to provide that service. Despite all of our difficulties, I feel that our station has ended up with one of the best dive units on the planet. I have two surface-supply teams on every watch 24 hours a day, 365 days a year. They're able to do full penetration diving, dive in contaminated environments and enter submerged aircraft, capsized vessels and submerged cars. They know how to assess the risks and how to stabilize these situations, and we teach other agencies what we've learned about this kind of diving. It has been like the tale of the phoenix rising from the ashes where this team is concerned. We went through some dog days in the 1990s because we were so stretched on a national basis for resources, but I really do believe that we're in good health today.

Sea Island is the only Coast Guard station in Canada equipped with a search and rescue dive team. On standby 24 hours a day, 365 days a year, two dive teams are capable of performing full penetration dives on submerged aircraft, vessels or vehicles. Like any other unit of the Canadian Coast Guard, these divers spend a great deal of time practising rescue scenarios; Kelly Alendal, a rescue specialist at the Sea Island station, has coached many of these exercises.
Courtesy Canadian Coast Guard, Pacific Region

whole gamut on this mission. We'd been tasked to help people, we saved lives and we lost lives. It's very rare in any Coast Guard in the world on one mission to search, save lives, try to intervene to resuscitate a life and still bring home people in a bag.

Thirteen years ago I started the Canadian Amphibious Search Team, CAST. Basically it was organized because too many times I had seen families of lost loved ones left empty-handed, without a body. I thought that not only do I work with professions who can help to solve missions, but I know of other agencies where people would like to get involved. We created a team that trained once a week and went on missions on the weekends. The majority of our team was divers, but we also had climbers, pilots, police officers, fire fighters, doctors, military, Coast Guard and technicians. We would go into areas only when other agencies had terminated their cases. Eighty percent of the time we were successful in finding the person in that search area.

We did get paid, but eight times out of ten we didn't ask for a cent. Whenever it got out of hand, say if I had to organize fifteen people to take a weekend off to go to Revelstoke or Prince Rupert, we had to have expenses covered. I ended up creating the Omega Foundation, which is a non-profit group that works by donations. If we knew of a family that was missing a loved one, we would go and do the operation regardless, but if the family wanted to pay us later or give a small donation to the foundation, that was great. We are still active today.

CHAPTER THREE

Night and Day, Every Day

BC Coast Pilots

"I was on a Chinese ship going into the Alcan dock at Kitimat, and I said to the captain as we approached the berth that I wanted to slow down, and he should put one shackle outside the hawse pipe. He said, 'Yes.' I asked him if he understood. 'Yes.' I told him to put the one shackle out, just walk it out and do it. 'Yes.' We were getting in closer and closer, but we weren't slowing down. The anchor should have been fenching up [catching bottom] by that time. I contacted one of the tugs and asked him which way the chain was leading on the anchor. He said, 'What anchor?' The anchor wasn't out! I said, 'Captain, put the anchor out!' He said, 'Yes.' He didn't understand a word I was saying."

Captain Rick Stanley, BC Coast Pilot

Pilot boats play a key role in transporting coast pilots to and from any commercial ship over three hundred and fifty tonnes that is visiting a BC port. Coast pilots truly are master seamen. They must have years of experience as master of deck watch aboard a ship before even contemplating the rigorous exams that will test their understanding of everything from tides and currents to bridge instruments and tugboat operations.

Dave Roels photo/PPA

By law, all ships over 350 gross registered tonnes entering BC coastal waters must be piloted into and out of port by an officer provided by the Pacific Pilotage Authority. "You could imagine what would happen if any foreign-going ship was allowed to wander around Canadian ports without knowledge of the local waters," comments pilot boat Captain Doug Riley. "The crew may be fine seamen, but they don't know the local currents or tides." *Each of the pilots under contract to the Authority has qualified for the job by years of experience as the master or the person in charge of the deck watch on board a ship, followed by courses and exams to demonstrate his knowledge of such things as tides and currents, dredged channel widths and lengths, cable locations, anchorage areas, aids to navigation, bridge signals and clearances, seamanship and shiphandling, the use of navigation and bridge instruments, chart work, the operation and interpretation of radar, docking procedures, the use of anchors and the operation of tugboats.*

Pilot boats are easily identified by the red and white flag that always flies from their highest point. BC has over 24,000 kilometres (15,000 miles) of coastline and over thirty shipping ports. Every commercial ship over 350 tonnes must be piloted into port by a professional coast pilot.

Courtesy BC Coast Pilots Association

At the present time there are 104 pilots working the coast night and day, 365 days a year. They are delivered to and disembarked from the ships by pilot boats, planes or helicopters, and they are always, according to Captain Riley, "immaculately dressed in suit and tie, though sometimes during the summer you might see one with an open collar." Veteran pilot Captain Alan Stanley points out that you can tell when a pilot is aboard because "a red and white vertically halved flag always flies from the ship's highest point."

"Pilots' salaries are based on a formula that includes their time aboard ship and the draft of the vessel," Captain Stanley explains. "Each pilot carries a bundle of source cards that he is required to fill out with the name of the ship and all its particulars, where and when he boarded and disembarked, and he hands these cards in to the Pilotage Authority, which pays the pilots their percentage of that source card. Shipping agents pay the Pilotage Authority for our services and then charge the shipping companies."

Incoming ships must notify the Authority of their estimated time of arrival at one of the pilot boarding stations on the coast and confirm that time a few hours before their actual arrival. Pilot boarding stations are located at five points on the coast: at Fairway Buoy, off Brotchie Ledge near Victoria; off Cape Beale at the entrance to Trevor Channel in Barkley Sound; off Triple Island near Prince Rupert; off Pine Island at the northwest end of Queen Charlotte Strait; and off Sand Heads at the mouth of the Fraser River.

Seen on the bridge of a cargo ship, Captain Alan Stanley is on duty as a BC Coast Pilot. Pilots are almost always immaculately dressed in a suit and tie.
Courtesy Captain Alan Stanley

Captain Alan Stanley was a well-known and highly respected member of BC's seafaring community. He worked on tugboats for many years before joining the cadre of highly skilled mariners who provide pilotage to seagoing ships on this coast. His brother Peter and his nephew Rick are also pilots. Captain Stanley served as a BC Coast Pilot from May 1, 1967, to May 1, 1997. He passed away in July 2007.

On most vessels the pilot's job is to give steering advice. He doesn't deal with the actual controls or the helm except on certain occasions, such as if he's having some difficulty relaying what he wants done, maybe because of language problems or because the commands are not always carried out. And sometimes there might be differences of opinion between the master and the pilot about what needs to be done. Therefore on a few occasions he is required to do some of the handling of the vessel himself. Then, instead of giving orders, he's

Commercial cargo ships can be as long as two city blocks and carry upwards of one-and-a-half million litres of fuel. Coast pilots use their years of experience to guide these vessels into port without grounding on any underwater shoals or colliding with other vessels.

Courtesy BC Coast Pilots Association

working hands-on, but that doesn't happen too often. It depends on the size of the vessel, too. Sometimes on a little vessel it's easier to do the steering yourself. You're getting what you want and it makes it easier for everyone. Then the master usually stands by in case you want to get away from the controls while you're steering on a straight course. Most of the time the master is in favour of it. I remember boarding a small cattle ship at one o'clock in the morning up at Goodwin and Johnson at Second Narrows and there were only the skipper and me in the wheelhouse all the way to Brotchie Ledge off Vancouver Island. He went down to the galley and made us Danish open-face sandwiches. We just talked and did the whole thing practically by ourselves. The rest of the crew were either sleeping or involved in some ship business.

The first year I was piloting I got dispatched to a vessel out of Nanaimo and had to take it to sea at Brotchie Ledge. The vessel was heavily loaded with lumber and was down by the head a little bit when we started out, but it's the general practice that, after they finish loading and get under way, the crew trim the ship up by filling the aft peak tank with seawater to put the ship on a more even keel. We were coming down the Haro Straits, nearing Discovery Island, when we found that the steering wasn't acting properly. The helmsman got about ten degrees starboard helm on the ship and it wouldn't come off, and the ship started to sheer off toward Discovery Island. Panic stations were all over. The captain was onto the engine room trying to find out what was wrong but none of them knew. Consequently I said that we were just going to have to go astern and stop the ship because she was just going to peel off and hit the island. This move was fine with the captain but the real objection came from the chief engineer—he didn't want to stop his engine on heavy bunker fuel because it congeals when the engine stops. They need one hour's notice of such a manoeuvre so that they can switch over to diesel fuel. But on this occasion the engineer had no alternative—he would have to flush the engine out with diesel fuel before the engine really cooled down. So after some screaming and hollering we got her going full astern and then got stopped, and the tide was ebbing so we gradually drifted out away from the island. We put out an anchor and a couple of shackles. There are fifteen fathoms of chain between each shackle. When we started to fench up we slacked out a lot more chain so that she would hang up while we found out why she had lost her steering.

It was a while before they discovered that, before we had left Nanaimo, someone had been in the room where the steering motor is located. In order to get in there, he had had to go through a manhole. When he came back out, he didn't reseal the manhole, so when the crew started filling the aft peak tank to trim the ship, it had overflowed into the steering room, submerging the electric motor under salt water. The steering happened to be at ten degrees starboard helm when it cut out. We were anchored there for twenty-four hours while they pumped out the aft peak tank and the steering room. They washed the motor out with fresh water, sealed it up, dried it off and started it again. Finally we left and they dropped me off at Brotchie Ledge.

Sometime in the early 1980s I was piloting on one of the early Greek cruise ships, the *Orpheus,* and the young master was very nervous. He imposed certain restrictions, one of them being never to use Active Pass between Mayne and Galiano Islands. As far as I was concerned his vessel was small enough and manoeuvrable enough that there was no question about its ability to use the Pass, but he made it so clear that instead of just saying, "No, you can't use Active Pass," he had actually taken a pen and blanked out everything on the chart between the two islands to indicate to pilots that Active Pass didn't exist. It was not there.

He also got so nervous any time he was going to go alongside a berth that he wanted to stop the engine and would pull back on the telegraph. In order to stop this jiggling on the telegraph, I'd sometimes have to put my hand on it and hold it. Then he'd put his hands on top of mine and try to direct which way he wanted to go until we got alongside the pier. Then everything would be fine. He was a good gentleman but just a very nervous one.

Once, as I was piloting a ship out of Vancouver and we were getting down south of East Point on Saturna Island, the mate came to me and said, "We've got a problem." I thought it was a mechanical problem and he wanted to stop the engine, but that wasn't it. One of the crew had brought a woman aboard in Vancouver but she hadn't got off when we departed and they didn't know how to get rid of her. The mate asked if we could get a pilot boat to take her off, but we couldn't do that as they're just for pilots. So I told him that I would make arrangements for a tug to come alongside and she could get off onto that. I called an Island Tug to come and they came out and took the lady off. There was some conversation that went on later between the crew member and the master regarding payment.

One time I left Roberts Bank on a fully loaded coal ship and as we were getting down near Discovery Island we detected a vessel going up along San Juan Island. I acquired this vessel—if you see something when you're navigating you "acquire" it—and got its CPA. This is a term used in radar navigation to mean "closest possible approach." When you're plotting a course, you always figure out what the CPA is going to be of any vessel you acquire, but the new Automatic Radar Plotting Aid (ARPA) radars are able to acquire the vessel you are interested in and give you its speed, its CPA, and all the information you require. First it looked as if this vessel would carry on up San Juan Island, but then I saw his vector, which is the direction of actual travel of the vessel, and by the readout from the ARPA I could see that he was changing course. Now he was heading straight toward us. We watched him for a while and figured he would change course eventually. We couldn't change course because we were doing twelve knots with the tide behind us. Meanwhile, the target kept getting closer and closer and closer. Finally it got to the stage where I had to do something. I told the captain that we had to take evasive action. We stopped engines, but going at that speed with such a heavy vessel there was no way we could stop the propeller from turning and no way we could go astern. There was nothing we could do. All the time the vessel was coming closer. We were downsizing the scale on the radar screen, going from six-mile range down to bare minimum, and when we picked the vessel up again, we could see it was carrying on in the same direction it had been going. Obviously it was operating on a GPS, and he was coming near our mountain of a ship without really knowing it was there. Of course, we'd been blowing the whistle constantly, and I guess maybe he finally heard the whistle and changed direction slightly, but he was right on top of us by that time. We both carried on. It's really scary, you know, for most mariners if an approaching vessel is just using the GPS on low visibility. They have a destination and a line they can follow to it on their GPS, but they're unaware of what other traffic is operating on that course. It kind of scares the daylights out of you.

Most small vessel owners are not out to commit suicide, however. Sometimes they're curious, and they just want to come over to wave to you as they go by. It's fine if you know what they're going to be doing, if they're going to be just giving a wave to you. That's okay. But you don't know that. And our angle of sight from the bridge to the water is a long way ahead. On the huge container ships it could be as much as half-a-kilometre away, and on the smaller freighters we can't see a small pleasure craft if it is even less than that.

Going in and out of English Bay it gets a little touchy at times. My eldest daughter, Alana, was into sailing. At one time she was very

Many cargo ships have as little as two metres (six feet) of clearance when they pass beneath the Lions Gate Bridge on their way to and from Vancouver Harbour, but despite this, pilots must keep the vessel at a brisk pace to push through the strong eddies that swirl beneath the bridge.
Courtesy BC Coast Pilots Association

Captain Alan Stanley was given this photo as a memento of Christmas 1969, which he spent aboard the Russian ship *Orsha*. An inscription on the back of the photo reads, "Mr. W.A. Stanley, our respected pilot in the memory of the joint evening party."

Courtesy Captain Alan Stanley

involved in Hobie Cat sailing and was out every Sunday on English Bay. One Sunday I was coming out of Vancouver on a Japanese ship heading to an anchorage in the outer harbour. Little sailboats were all over the place. I said to the captain that I'd better watch out because my daughter was out there someplace. I no sooner got the words out of my mouth than I could hear coming from the water "Hi Dad!" There she was, right beside the ship, sailing around. She knew I was working.

I spent one New Year's Eve on the *Orsha,* a Russian ship. We left Rupert heading for Triple Island about eleven o'clock in the morning and got the tide coming out by Watson Island. After that the ship was heading to Tahsis. The captain said, "Pilot, we will have New Year's dinner about eight o'clock tonight, so we will just have a light lunch." I got to Triple Island and was finished work—the pilot dead-heads to five miles outside Nootka Sound—and the ship kept on down Hecate Strait. Later they came and invited me for New Year's dinner in the lounge. At the officer's table were the captain, the woman doctor, the engineer and I. The rest of the crew was all scattered at tables around the lounge, except for those on duty. They had

St. Nikolas and his helpers, all dressed up in St. Nikolas attire, and they had presents and gave me a paper sack with some Russian candies in it and also a little bottle of vodka. We all had dinner and then afterwards they started dancing in the lounge. One of the seamen came over and asked me if I would dance and I said no. He asked the doctor next to me and she got up and danced with him. It was just ordinary dancing, no Russian stuff. Then she came back to the table and asked me if I would dance. I didn't want to insult anybody so we had a short dance on the deck, though the ship had a slight roll that made it a bit difficult for the footing. That was a nice New Year's Eve. I got to know that captain very well, Captain Tabakar, and we'd see each other periodically throughout the years.

For pilots the method of boarding and disembarking ships is by a rope ladder that is draped over the side of the vessel, and when you

At one time, coast pilots boarded commercial vessels by way of a ladder that was pulled up to the deck mechanically. This method, however, proved to be very unsafe as the cables could easily be twisted by even a small gust of wind. The International Marine Pilots' Association finally outlawed mechanical ladders, and today coast pilots board and disembark using the ancient technology of rope ladders.
Courtesy BC Coast Pilot Association

get off or on the ladder you're at about the same level as the deck of the boat that delivers you to your ship. The requirement is that the pilot must not have to climb any more than thirty feet from the pilot boat to the deck of the vessel. This means, for example, that the big coal carriers, because they're so high, have to rig an accommodation ladder in conjunction with the rope ladder to reach the ship's deck. The pilot ladders are rigged so that about every ten feet they have spreader bars that extend about six feet wide to eliminate the ladder twisting. Sometimes when a wind comes up, it has a tendency to lift the ladder away from the ship and turn it over on top of you. That used to happen periodically. For a while they tried mechanical ladders. We then had only about ten feet of real pilot ladder and they had machinery on deck that would pull this ladder up to the deck level. The problem was that the cable that was taking that section of ladder up would twist and the cable would cross over itself. Finally a law came in from the International Marine Pilots' Association that the mechanical ladders had to be abandoned on all ships. They were not very safe.

A friend of mine, Captain Ed Sonne, came into the pilots just about six months before I did. One day he was disembarking from a Russian container ship at Brotchie Ledge. It was quite a distance down—about thirty feet from the ship's deck—and they had a few stairs up from the deck to the top of the bulwarks, two handrails over the bulwarks and then the pilot ladder down the side of the ship. Ed had gone up these stairs on the inboard side of the bulwarks and had turned to face the ladder to go down it when one of the handrails over the bulwarks carried away, flew off and landed in the water. He couldn't hang on and fell down, landing on top of the pilot boat. He was killed instantly. One of his sons now operates a pilot boat out of Steveston at Sand Heads.

After this happened, the Pilotage Authority and the pilots agreed that when the pilot vessel came to pick up or let off a pilot it would sit off a ways until he was down or up, or at least at a reasonable distance on the ladder, and the boat could slide in underneath him and pick him up. Then if the pilot should fall off the ladder he would hit the water, not the pilot vessel.

When I was on the tugboats, we used to go down the Columbia River quite frequently and the river pilots there got to know us. One of them was Bob Morrison, and he and I became close friends. One time he was coming down the river with a loaded log ship and they were changing pilots at Astoria where the Columbia River bar pilots

Captain Harold Monks descends the pilot's ladder to board the pilot boat in 2001. The International Marine Pilots' Association states that a pilot must not climb more than nine metres (thirty feet) from pilot boat to cargo vessel.

Courtesy Captain Harold Monks

Both the pilot boat captain and the coast pilot hope for calm weather as they pull up alongside the vessel. Ultimately, the captain must decide whether the conditions are safe enough for the delivery or pickup of the coast pilot.

Courtesy International Maritime Pilots Association

take over to take vessels out into the ocean. They deal with the area from Astoria out to the lightship, which is about eighteen miles. When the bar pilot came up to the bridge to relieve him, the new pilot told Bob to be careful with the ladder because it was kind of short of the deck of the pilot vessel and it was a long way down. The pilot ladder started on top of the load of logs on the deck of the ship, and Bob began working his way along them to come down the ladder. He was on the pilot ladder but still on the pile of logs—hadn't even reached the side of the ship—when the whole works carried away. He and the pilot ladder landed on the deck of the pilot vessel. The only thing that saved his life was the fact that the pilot vessel had a false deck with grating on the top of it, so that when he fell on it the whole thing collapsed. But he was smashed up real bad and never came back to piloting.

The harbour at Tasu, a mine on the west coast of the Queen Charlottes, opens up quite wide but its entrance is very small and hard to detect from the ocean side. Sometimes, when the ships were incapable of entering the harbour, they'd have to go up to Triple Island, board pilots there and then come down and enter into Tasu. And when the ship departed Tasu, it would have to go back to Triple Island to drop the pilot off. Other times a helicopter was used to fly pilots out of Sandspit so they could meet the ship and board her about five miles out at sea. Then we'd pilot the ship into Tasu and tie her up alongside the berth there. The helicopter would land on the deck of the ship and we could just walk down to it, board it and fly back into Sandspit. Later another pilot would be brought in to take the ship out. Before they started to use helicopters, we used to fly in on fixed-wing aircraft from Sandspit to Tasu and back. It was really scary at times with the weather conditions what they are there. Obviously helicopters were real time-savers.

I guess one of the most difficult places for boarding on and off vessels was out at Cape Beale on the west coast of Vancouver Island. There was a pilot vessel there that had extremely good operators. I know we came out of Tahsis one trip and it was on the borderline whether we could disembark off Cape Beale or have to go inside the inlet, board off and then direct the ship out to sea again. The wind was blowing real hard, a heavy southwest swell moving in with a wind blowing southeast, one against the other. The ship had to keep up enough speed but would try and make a lee for the pilot vessel to come alongside. If it went too slowly, everything was rolling, but it couldn't go too fast either, so the pilot boat came alongside and was riding up and down the side of the ship. You try to find the moment when the waves subside a bit and the pilot boat sits still, allowing you to make your attempt from the ladder to the pilot vessel. Pilot boat crews are so important. Your life depends on them, and their first concern is your safety. They do one heck of a job. They tell you when it's too tough and they can't do it.

Captain Harold Beck spent eighteen years on tugboats, a year deep sea and twenty-five-and-a-half years as a BC coast pilot. Since his retirement in 1989 he has been a member of the Ancient Mariners group and the Canadian Merchant Service Guild Pioneers Association of retired officers, and he continues to celebrate his Norwegian heritage by attending the regular meetings at the Sons of Norway in Victoria.

I wrote the pilots exam in 1962. I was number seven on the waiting list and had to wait until enough people retired or died before I was taken on, so I wasn't called to be a pilot until March 1, 1964. The best move I ever made. The first ship I piloted was an old Greek one with a single rudder and twin propellers. Backing out of berth South A at Ogden Point, Victoria, I decided to get the stern off the dock by

Captain Harold Beck served as a BC coast pilot for nearly twenty-six years. He retired in 1989 but remains committed to the profession through his membership in the Canadian Merchant Service Guild Pioneers Association of retired officers.
Courtesy Harold Beck

A ship's propeller may measure six metres (twenty feet) and weigh several tonnes.
Courtesy BC Coast Pilots Association

putting stern power on the port engine, then stopping it and putting half-astern on the starboard engine. But the starboard engine wouldn't start. The small assist tug could not hold the stern of the ship from swinging in toward the breakwater, so I had to kick the port engine ahead to keep the stern of the ship off the breakwater. Then I had the tug move to the starboard bow to push and kick the port engine forward and astern until we cleared the berth. So went my first job.

In my early days as a pilot most of our transportation was by bus. In some places we had to take a bus and then a taxi to the dock. Even when we had to travel between Vancouver and Vancouver Island we had to take a bus and ferry, and sometimes because of the bus schedule we had to wait around for three hours before the ship sailed. The only time we could take an aircraft was first thing in the morning or last thing at night. It was helpful if our wives could drive us. The whole travelling thing was very time inefficient, and eventually we pilots formed our own company and arranged for better transportation to and from the ships by taxi and aircraft. One time two of us had to fly to Terrace, but they had trouble with the aircraft, so by the time we were able to board another plane and take off, Terrace airport was closed for the night and we had to fly into Smithers. Our ship was due to sail from Kitimat at midnight so I sent a note forward to the plane's pilot and asked him to pre-order a taxi for us. It was there when we arrived and I told the driver that this would be a charge to the Pacific Pilotage Authority. He called his dispatcher who told him they wouldn't accept that. So I suggested a Visa. They wouldn't accept that either. Finally they agreed to accept my personal cheque. That's how we arrived in Kitimat in time for our ship, which, as it turned out, was delayed until six the next morning.

Sometimes we did have language trouble on the bridge of foreign ships with crews that couldn't understand English, but on most ships there is usually a small blackboard on the bridge for writing down the course to be steered. It's there to remind the helmsmen. I used it when altering course and I would indicate port or starboard with my arm and point my finger on the rudder indicator dial to let them know how many degrees of rudder I wanted. On the better quality ships they would have a three-decagon that sat in a three-case pocket with nine sides and one side exposed. The decagon had numbers from zero to nine, and you'd spin it around to the number to show the new course you wanted and then indicate the rudder position on the dial.

Captain Beck's wife, Memory: "In 1964, when Harold was a pilot, the Greek ship he was dispatched to was to be moved from Chemainus to Crofton, so my husband suggested we drive to Chemainus. I would drop him there and pick him up at Crofton. I took along our baby, who was six or seven months old. When my husband spoke to the captain he found out that the ship's departure was delayed for a few hours. As it was lunchtime, he invited me aboard for lunch and said that the crew hadn't been home for a year and would I bring the baby on board and let the crewmen hold him. I wasn't sure about that, but Harold said okay. The men passed the baby around and some of them were so affected they were crying, probably thinking of their own children they hadn't seen for a year."

On one occasion departing from the grain berth in Prince Rupert, I told the quartermaster at the helm "hard to port." I had a small tugboat pushing the ship's bow off the berth, and without checking on the rudder position, I gave an engine movement of dead slow ahead to move the ship's stern off the berth. Instead, I heard a loud squealing noise. I said to stop engine and went to check the rudder indicator. It was hard to starboard instead of port. Incidents do happen if you don't keep a check on everything that's going on.

On two occasions after entering Vancouver Harbour to berth freighters—once at Ballantyne Pier and the other time at Lapointe Pier—I had an instinct that there was something wrong. Sure enough, after stopping the main engine power the engineers were unable to start it again, so there was no astern or ahead power for berthing. On both occasions I had to have the freighters towed into their berths.

The role of specialized ship-berthing tugs is to move the vessels into and away from their berths. Here the *Shoryu Maru* is pushed into position at a Vancouver dock by able tugboats a fraction of its size.

Courtesy BC Coast Pilots Association

One Christmas Eve another pilot and I joined the *Hongkong Clipper* or the *Honor*—I can't remember which—at port. What I do remember about it were the cockroaches in the wheelhouse, cabins and everywhere you looked. The Chinese skipper told us that he had bought a little turkey and we'd have it after we cleared Cape Beale on our way to Kitimat. His girlfriend was on the ship, too, but she got seasick and went to bed. So the three of us sat in the lounge eating bits of turkey and having a drink of Scotch. When we arrived in Kitimat on Boxing Day they wouldn't berth us until the next day so we had to stay aboard one more night. Lying in my bunk, I saw cockroaches all around me; they were even running across my chest at times. But they say if the cockroaches die, there's sickness aboard. One of these ships ran aground and had to go into the shipyard for repairs but there were so many rats aboard it the shipyard crew walked off. The quarantine officer had to go aboard and put out rat poison. I told him that I usually ate only rice when aboard one of those ships. He said, "You wouldn't have eaten the rice if you had seen the rice bin."

One time aboard a German ship the captain ordered coffee brought to the bridge. After it came in a porcelain jug, I poured coffee into my cup and a cockroach dropped into it. The captain went up one side of the steward and down the other. I don't think he forgot that tongue-lashing.

But it wasn't only on the deep-sea ships that we ran into vermin. When I was on one of the tugs, we found cockroaches in the galley behind a meat block that was bolted to the bulkhead. We used a steam hose to see if that would get rid of them, but it didn't. We eventually had the galley sealed off and fumigated. The cook we had was not the cleanest person. He'd be making bread buns, mixing up the dough, and he'd be sweating, wipe his face and forehead with his hands, then put back them back in the dough. The bread buns did taste okay, though.

Jack Kirkham and I were on the bridge of the cruise ship M.V. *Rotterdam* as pilots, steaming south in Hecate Strait for Vancouver, when we heard a distress call from the *Princess Royal* that she was sinking off Cape St. James and they were abandoning her. Jack set up an intercept course on the chart and we headed in that direction. I understood that it was a charter boat out of Seattle carrying research people from UBC. A Canadian Aurora aircraft came over us on the same course but the overcast was so low that it didn't spot them. Some hours later when Jack and I had gone down to have lunch, we heard the passengers yelling, "There they are!" Two inflatable rafts loaded with people were in the water on the ship's starboard side.

The skipper of the *Rotterdam* was going to put a boat over, but it was too rough and he changed his mind when the boat slammed into the ship's side. After we spotted the survivors, three helicopters—one Canadian and two American—came from Sandspit to pick them up. They had been waiting for a position to pick up survivors. While we were waiting, the tug *Haida Monarch* and a forty-one-foot sailboat under storm-sail showed up. Air Sea Rescue ignored the sailboat, but if the helicopters had been unable to come, that sailboat would have had an easier job doing the rescue than us because of his freeboard, which was probably no more than three feet. Then we could have steamed to windward of the two rafts, giving them some protection while he did the rescue.

I joined a smaller cruise ship, the *Northwest Explorer,* at Hardy Bay on Vancouver Island. Maurice Johansen was the pilot already on board, and we dropped him at Westview on our way to Princess Louisa Inlet. When we arrived there, the skipper decided to put the Zodiac in the water to check on the tidal current in the narrow channel entrance. The ship was about 170 feet long and had 160 passengers, fairly large to transit the narrows but it had made it the trip before. However, I think that passage had scared the old man a bit. I told him that if he took the time to check the current, we would miss the slack water, but he wanted to be careful. By the time the Zodiac had checked on the current it was too late to make the transit. I turned the ship away from the entrance and anchored just off Malibu Island with the stern facing out, but after the current picked up, the ship's stern was facing in toward the island.

Meanwhile, the crew put the Zodiacs in the water for the passengers who wanted to go see the falls in Princess Louisa Inlet. I became nervous that the ship's stern was too close to the rocks off the island and knew that if the anchor dragged we would be in trouble. The Zodiacs would be gone for three to four hours, so we steamed across the channel [of Jervis Inlet] and found a good place to anchor four to five miles away. I had to put my head down for a couple of hours nap, and the skipper decided he would take a Zodiac, go ashore and have a look around. Later I went up to the wheelhouse and with binoculars saw a Zodiac with people in it coming toward the ship. Finally the old man came back with a bunch of wildflowers he had picked, and I told him about the Zodiac that was coming. We decided to pick up the anchor and head down toward Princess Louisa, but before we had the anchor up, the first Zodiac arrived. I was heading down below and met one of the passengers, but when I asked him how his trip had been he just scoffed. I went back up to the wheel-house and saw a second Zodiac coming. Then the social director who had gone ashore with them came up to the wheelhouse. She didn't say anything at first. The skipper told her that at dinner that evening he was going to tell the passengers what an enjoyable afternoon he'd had picking flowers. She grumped, "You're not going to tell them anything." We steamed to the entrance of Princess Louisa Inlet where the rest of the Zodiacs were waiting and learned that one of the Zodiac engines had broken down and the whole afternoon had fallen apart. As it was at the end of our voyage, we then headed for Vancouver. When steaming along Agamemnon Channel, I slowed to cut down on the wash because in the good old days there had usually been log booms tied up there. We came around a corner and right in front of us were a lot of fish farms. It was a good job I wasn't at full speed. We anchored just outside of Buccaneer Bay, then left early the next morning for Vancouver.

About six o'clock one morning I was travelling south in Principe Channel aboard the *Royal Princess* when the fog started closing in, so I put the whistle on. The captain came marching out of his room wanting to know what was going on. I told him that there were fishermen out there in the fog. He shut the foghorn off then went back to his room. Not even five minutes had gone by before he came back out and turned it on again. He had had second thoughts about his actions.

A life at sea is not the best when you are married. You miss a lot of events, though mostly your loving wife and children. Looking back at my life at sea, there were days of boredom, but overall I would not have stayed if I didn't like the sea. It has a call of freedom that I believe has been lost in today's world. Instead of the captain, the office wants to be the master of the ship.

Captain Harold Monks began his seafaring years working on Imperial Oil tankers along the BC coast, then went deep sea on Norwegian ships. Over the years he kept upgrading his certification and worked on many different vessels, including Fisheries patrol boats. In his final twenty-three years at sea, from 1979 to his retirement in 2002, he served as a BC coast pilot. He lives on his picturesque family homestead in Tofino, BC, overlooking the sea.

Captain Harold Monks served as a BC coast pilot for twenty-three years. Here he is seen on a Netherlands tanker, the *Sericata*.

Courtesy Captain Harold Monks

While I was in the pilots, after exiting Quatsino Sound on a trip from Port Alice to Vancouver, we ran into a real howler. We didn't get an updated weather report until just before reaching the entrance of the sound, and that's when we learned storm- to hurricane-force winds were forecast during the night. The ship was only partially loaded so it offered a lot of resistance to the wind. Off Lawn Point at the entrance to the sound, ten miles from Cape Cook, I turned the navigation over to the officer on watch. I would take over again off Victoria. I went to bed, and although there was some shaking during the night, slept reasonably well. After getting up, I went to the bridge and had a look at the chart and found we were still just off Solander Island at Cape Cook. We had done no more than a couple of knots [two miles an hour] at full rpm during the night when it had been blowing hurricane-force [over seventy miles an hour]. Some of the ship's antennas and insulators had blown off their mountings, and the storm had damaged the wind indicator and light on Solander Island and put them out of commission.

Those winds reminded me of a trip on the Norwegian ship *Ternefjell* in the North Atlantic where we were bucking into a huge sea. For three days we were at a standstill. To hold our position we had to head directly into it, and if the helmsman lost steerage by as little as three or four degrees, we had to phone the engine room for extra revolutions to keep our bow into it and prevent the ship being blown beam-on to the sea.

It was often a mystery what sort of a meal we were going to be served up on the bridge on one of the foreign ships. Often they asked you what you'd like to eat, and I would tell them that I would prefer the same food as they had. Particularly on the Korean ships, they'd think they could do one better and almost always they would come up with a thin steak, french fries, and shredded cabbage with a blob of mayonnaise on top. They think that we don't like their food and seem to believe that this is standard western cuisine. One Christmas Day on a Korean ship, the captain said, "Oh, this is a special day. We'll have to bring some special food up." So for his special Christmas dinner for me, the captain brought up a hamburger that he'd bought a few days before in San Francisco. It was from a hamburger machine, sealed in cellophane, accompanied by a tin of peaches. This was my special meal. When no one was looking, I walked over to the wing of the bridge and threw it over the side. When you get older, missing out on a meal is probably good for the waistline.

Nothing is routine in the pilots. The last job I had before I retired in 2002 was on a Cypriot-registered ship with Greek owners. I had to take the ship from the Victoria Pilot Boarding Station to Van Wharves on the north side of Vancouver Harbour. So often I've found these Cypriot ships to be the worst of the worst, pretty scruffy. The third mate was up on the bridge with me, a big fellow who didn't say much, and when I spoke to him he didn't seem to understand. I found out later that he was Ukrainian. The fellow steering was a Filipino. As we headed up the Strait of Georgia, I could see a fog bank off the Fraser River, so I told the mate that he should take precautions such as getting another seaman as lookout on the bridge, getting two radar sets operating and advising the engine room to reduce speed. The engine room needed twenty minutes' warning to change over from heavy to light fuel in order to reduce speed, but the mate didn't seem to understand that he had to call the engine room. As we got into the fog, I told him to switch on the ship's whistle in the auto mode. He didn't understand, had no idea how to do it. I guess he'd never had to use it. Eventually we got the whistle blowing and managed to slow down just before getting into quite a bit of traffic off the Fraser River. The fog was quite thick all the way up until we got to First Narrows Bridge [Lions Gate Bridge]. That's when the captain appeared. We got into the narrows and were going to make a turn to prepare for a starboard landing at the dock. I said, "Slow astern." Nothing happened. She wouldn't go astern. There was a tug standing by and it helped us to manoeuvre into the berth. We are usually prepared for situations like this. Generally we notify the Vessel Traffic System controller on the VHF about a problem, in this case engine failure, and they arrange for a steamship inspector to come down. We also have to fill out a notation on the usual form for the pilot office so that the next pilot on the ship will know that there's been a problem. As I was filling out the form with my derogatory comments, I could sense someone behind me. I turned around and there was the captain, a big Greek with a gift, a bottle of Scotch. All pilots have had these types of experiences, but I remember this one vividly as it was my last job, and in a way it imprinted on me the worth of being a pilot. It was an interesting farewell.

Captain Rick Stanley remembers as a boy always being on the water with his father and grandfather. Three of his uncles were fishermen and two were on tugboats. He left school at the age of seventeen and joined Vancouver Tugs, where his uncles worked. As a deckhand he found himself doing the dirty jobs like washing toilets, so in 1972 at the age of twenty-

two he decided to go back to school to get his tugboat master's ticket. He has been a fisherman, worked on tugboats belonging to Westminster Tugs, Kingcome Navigation and Seaspan. He has also worked in the Arctic for Arctic Transportation Ltd. and is currently an enthusiastic BC coast pilot.

I decided to write my pilot's exam in 1987 and got licensed in 1990. I've been in the pilots now for fifteen years, and in all of the jobs I've had, I've never had so much fun as I do in piloting right now. Shiphandling is such a thrill and it's a big thing I look forward to.

Before I wrote the pilot's exam, I was an observer on a ship to see what the job was all about. I went out with Captain Bob Read to board the ship at Cape Beale. The seas were really high, and Bob asked Doug Riley, captain of the pilot boat, what he thought about the safety of boarding the ship. It was rolling really heavily and going up and down. I thought that if I wanted to be a pilot, I had better follow Captain Read up the ladder, so as we came near enough I just grabbed the ladder and the pilot boat took off. The deckhand was yelling, "Good one!" And I was thinking, oh yeah! But I made it. I found out from that experience that you always watch the movement of the ship and the pilot boat, grab hold when the pilot boat is highest up the ladder and get your first three steps in as quickly as possible. That means that there's less ladder to climb but also, if you get on real low and the pilot boat comes near, you could get pinned between the boat and the ship. Once you make up your mind to go you don't hesitate, because the situation will change quickly.

Coming down the pilot ladder, I prefer to use the manropes. They are two ropes outside the ladder that you can hang on to as you're going down. You can use your hands to brake yourself. Especially in a heavy sea with the pilot boat going up and down, you can time yourself so that when the pilot boat comes up you're right there and can jump on still holding onto the manropes as a guide. I find it a lot safer to use them.

There are good reasons why pilots must have a lot of experience plus a master's ticket. We must be able to make difficult decisions and work our way through problems. In my early days as a pilot I was on an ore ship out of Campbell River and I had five little tugs assisting to get me off the berth. There were so many sports fishermen around us that I asked the tugs to go and chase the small boats away because we were coming out. The problem was that, as soon as one was chased away, another one would come in. I decided to go anyway. I

Captain Rick Stanley was a tugboat master for many years and became a licensed coast pilot in 1990. Shiphandling is a thrill from which he has yet to tire.
Courtesy Captain Rick Stanley

let all the lines go, blew the whistle. They were all still fishing away, so as we started pushing away from the berth, all of these little boats were sandwiching along the ship's side.

One problem I had in my first year as a pilot related to foreign crews not speaking English. I had a little Russian ship from Triple Island to put in to the ocean dock at Prince Rupert. When I got aboard the ship, I found that there was no English spoken, Russian only. All the equipment and radar directions were written in Russian. I would point to the telegraphs, surmising that green had to be ahead and red astern, and I pointed to port and starboard and pointed to the compass. That was how we got to Prince Rupert. When we approached the berth, I stopped engines and then went out on the bridge wing to watch. I'd run back in and point to starboard, run outside again, run in, point to the right on the telegraphs, run back out, run back in. That's how I made the landing.

Another trip, I was on a Chinese ship going into the Alcan dock at Kitimat, and I said to the captain as we approached the berth that I wanted to slow down, and he should put one shackle outside the hawse pipe. He said, "Yes." I asked him if he understood. "Yes." I told him to put the one shackle out, just walk it out and do it. "Yes." We were getting in closer and closer, but we weren't slowing down. The anchor should have been fenching up by that time. I contacted one of the tugs and asked him which way the chain was leading on the anchor. He said, "What anchor?" The anchor wasn't out. I said, "Captain, put the anchor out." He said, "Yes." He didn't understand a word I was saying. I decided that the only thing I could do was take it real slow and work my way in there. I do prefer the anchor, though.

Jim Brady, a good friend of mine, and I were both piloting the *Nordic Prince,* a Norwegian cruise ship. He was number one pilot and took the ship off the berth, but as soon as he did that, the gyro-compass failed, so we had no gyro. By rights we should have taken the ship out and anchored and had it fixed, but the weather was good, and we decided to head north to Alaska anyway so the ship would not be behind on its schedule. As a pilot you're doing visual sailing. You're on radar and using a magnetic compass for courses given. It was a neat trip up the Inside Passage even without a gyro. The old man was so pleased he gave us both a bottle of Chivas Regal Scotch.

Riley's Boat Service, based in Port Alberni, has ferried pilots to and from their ships in that area since 1936. Captain Doug Riley joined the family business in 1956 as a crewman and went on to run the company until 2003. During those years he experienced some horrific weather and rescues, and his reminiscences about old-timers and events provide much insight into the pilots' working lives. His story is part of BC coast history. He still lives in Port Alberni with his wife Mickey.

In 1936 my father, Reece, and my mother, Alice, started Riley's Boat Service at Port Alberni, and at that time ninety-eight percent of their work was going into Kildonan, Bamfield, Ucluelet and all up and down the inlet because there were no roads to access these places and very few float planes. Dad was kept busy just carrying pilots and other passengers and a small amount of freight. There was another operator, Blackmore, that had two speedboats in competition for the pilot boat service because up until 1946 the pilot could decide who he wanted to take him off the ship. When the Blackmore business closed, it was strictly my father that did the pilot boat work for the Cape Beale area. We've gone through a few boats, like the *Maureen R.*, which was his original pilot boat, and during the war years he purchased another called the *Black Hawk,* which had been a rum-runner. It was capable of doing up to forty-five knots if you opened it right up. He sold that after the war and kept on with the *Maureen R.*

Captain Reece Riley founded Riley's Boat Service in 1936 and ran it until he drowned in a violent storm off the west coast of Vancouver Island in 1950.
Courtesy Captain D. Riley

In 1950 he told my Mom that he was tired of going up and down the Alberni Canal with a spotlight on and his head out the window, looking for debris, and only doing eighteen to twenty knots. He wanted to get a slow boat where he could sit in the wheelhouse with a stove on down below and be nice and warm. He decided to go for a fishboat-type hull, which he purchased from Bill Osborne in Port Alberni who had just finished constructing it. So Dad had it launched in 1950 as the *R.E. Riley* and left to take his old boat, the *Maureen R.,* up to Port Alice to sell to Harry Hole Sr.. Then he was to return and operate the new *R.E. Riley.*

Captain Doug Riley was the owner of Riley's Boat Service, a Port Alberni company that has transported pilots to and from their ships since 1936.
Courtesy Captain D. Riley

He had been gone for five or six days and we hadn't heard from him. We were very anxious, hoping that he'd pulled in at some small cove waiting for the weather to subside. We heard later that he'd stopped at Tofino about four o'clock in the afternoon, and there had been a crack in the forward window where a wave had hit it. There was a southeast gale brewing at the time. He went up to the store to get dry matches because his matches had got wet, jumped back on his boat and took off, and no one ever saw him again. We had Rescue go out and they found parts of the boat. The engine was sitting on one of the reefs with the shaft in a U shape. He'd lost his life on the west coast in a violent storm.

Fortunately for our financial future, the pilots came to ask my mom if she would maintain the pilot boat service. She had been looking after the business part of it as manager and dispatcher, so we were very lucky. We hired Bill Johnson to operate the pilot boat for us, but in 1954 he decided he wanted to go into another line of work, surveying ships. We then hired Joe Quilty, an experienced mariner. After a while he approached my mother and pointed out that, since every trip was at least ten hours long and he was the only person on board, it was getting very tiring because we were getting a little more shipping all the time. I had no yen for the water once my father lost his life, but I agreed to help on the pilot boat for a six-month stint, starting September 1, 1956. I was twenty years old. That six months ended up being forty-eight years. Joe Quilty left in 1961 when I got my master's certificate, and my deckhand then was Fred Ursul. My mother retired in 1966, and my new wife, Mickey, and I took over the business, she managing the office and me running the boat. When I started, there were 48 pilots to cover the BC coast. Now there are 104.

Our pilot boat was like a taxi for the pilots. If we were boarding a pilot on a vessel that was coming from sea, stopping at Cape Beale before going on to, say, Tahsis, we would go off Cape Beale with the pilot. He would board the vessel up a Jacob's ladder, introduce himself to the captain, and they would take off for Tahsis. He didn't have to do anything on board until they came near Estevan Point, which is when he would take over, guide them inside, take the ship in to the dock and then grab a cab and head home. We'd also take pilots off vessels. Let's say another ship was leaving Tahsis where he had taken on a deck load, was full of cargo, and his destination was Hong Kong. The pilot would get on in Tahsis, take the ship out to Estevan Point, then I would pick up the pilot at Cape Beale and take him back to Port Alberni. Ships could also be going to Gold River, Port Alice, Tasu, Kitimat or Ocean Falls along the coast.

Alberni Inlet (formerly known as the Alberni Canal) on Vancouver Island is a long, narrow flute that leads forty kilometres (twenty-five miles) inland from the Pacific Ocean at Barkley Sound and the Broken Group Islands. The inlet can accommodate deep-sea vessels loading lumber products at the town of Port Alberni at the head of the inlet. Stiff winds often funnel down the inlet, but it took the Alaska earthquake of March 27, 1964—at 9.2 on the Richter scale, the most powerful earthquake in North American history—to cause real damage to the inlet and the town. Although the epicentre was 125 km east of Anchorage, the tsunami that travelled down the coast entered the inlet in four successive waves. The first, eight feet high, drained the inlet, leaving fishboats tipped on the bottom. The second wave, travelling at 240 miles per hour, damaged 375 homes and washed 55 more homes away. In spite of the devastation, there were no fatalities.

The Alaska earthquake of 1964, which measured 9.2 on the Richter scale, caused a tsunami that travelled the length of the BC coast. Port Alberni was slammed by four consecutive waves and the total cost of the damage was close to ten million dollars.
University of Washington Libraries, Special Collections, UW 17947

The *Ocean Ranger* was the biggest oil-drilling rig of its day, touted to be unsinkable and capable of drilling in areas too dangerous for other rigs. Built by Mitsubishi Heavy Industries of Japan, it was first operated in 1976 in the Bering Sea off Alaska. It moved from there to New Jersey, then Ireland, and in November 1980 arrived on the Grand Banks, 170 miles east of St. John's, Newfoundland.

On Sunday, February 14, 1982, a vicious storm developed south of Newfoundland, and by sunset winds were up to 90 knots and the seas were rapidly building. Around seven p.m. a massive wave, estimated to be over thirty metres (one hundred feet) high, crashed over the rig, smashing a porthole in the ballast control room. Water rushed in, shorting the circuits, and the rig began to list. At one a.m. the next morning the crew requested help from Search and Rescue and a half-hour later the crew took to the lifeboats. The Ocean Ranger disappeared from the Coast Guard's radar two hours later.

All eighty-four crew members died. Search teams were only able to locate twenty-two bodies, two lifeboats and six life rafts. A royal commission concluded that the rig had design flaws, particularly in the ballast control room, and that the crew lacked proper safety training and equipment.

We did have some hairy experiences off Cape Beale. In the earlier days, when you really think about it, as the operator of a pilot boat—and with the pilots' discretion, of course—there were times when we put pilots on and off ships that in some ways were very dangerous. I'm sure that if ninety percent of the pilots' wives had known the things that their husbands went through, they'd have told them to find another line of work. If I had had video pictures of some of their experiences, their wives would have shaken their heads.

For example, there was an oil rig called the *Ocean Ranger* that came into Port Alberni one time. It was coming down from Alaska and heading south around Cape Horn and then north again, but it had to come into Port Alberni to change its hydraulic anchor to electrical. Vancouver Shipyards were the main contractors for the work. Although the rig was self-propelled, the management hired a local tug to tow it into the channel because there was a pretty good swell outside that would have made boarding the pilots difficult. After it was a few miles into the inlet, we decided that it was calm enough to board the pilots.

To get on this rig wasn't like getting on a Jacob's ladder and climbing up the side of a ship. Instead there was a crane operator, Bill Dugas, who lowered a circular platform, about six feet in diameter, with rope lashings holding it up to the crane, and around the outside of this circle was a padded ring for the passenger to stand on. The pilots were to throw their bags into the centre of the platform, and then step onto the outer ring and hang onto the lashings. Then the crane operator would take them up to the rig's deck. The first pilot put his bag on, grabbed the lashings and stepped off our boat onto the ring. He was then lifted up to the rig. The second pilot, Gordie Barker, who was the biggest man in the outfit, had his bag in one hand, put one foot on the outer part and one hand on the lashings, but by now the swell had come up and we'd started dropping back. Before I could put our engine in forward, the platform was sliding off of our deck. So here he goes! He's hanging on with one hand and he can't grab hold with his other hand because he's holding his bag with it. He went swinging out, and I knew exactly where he was going to end up. I went full astern on the engines, and in about thirty seconds he dropped into the water. I took the boat out of gear. It seemed like minutes but it was probably only six or seven seconds before he finally came to the surface, and by that time my deckhand, Fred, and I were out on deck. Fred had a pike pole, gave the end to Gordie, then went around to the stern and jumped on the stern grid.

Fred was really anxious to get Gordie out of the water and asked him to take his hand. Gordie said, "Take it easy, Fred. I can get up there." We all started to laugh. He was fine, except for being wet—and he was still holding his bag. The shock never hit him until we got him home that night. The other pilot stayed with the *Ocean Ranger*.

After all the work was complete, we boarded the out-bound pilots and one of them had a new pair of gloves. He came off the pilot boat and grabbed the ladder. When we moved the boat away, his hands came out of his gloves, and he ended up to his waist in water hanging onto the ladder. We stood by while he got his foot on the bottom rung, but he was wet. That oil rig took over one hundred days to reach Newfoundland.

One instance from the early 1970s I always remember involved a pilot named Colin Wilson. He stood about five-foot-six or seven and only weighed about 115 pounds, but he was like a cat, very good on the ladder, the best among the pilots that I'd ever seen. We went out to this old Liberty ship and there was quite a sea running. Normally, with the way the weather was, we'd have gone up to the ship and told the captain that he was going to have to follow the pilot boat in past Seapool Rocks—which are about a mile and a half inside Cape

Built by Mitsubishi Heavy Industries of Japan in the 1970s, the *Ocean Ranger* was the largest oil drill of its time and was thought to be unsinkable. It began drilling in the Bering Sea in 1976 and worked its way around the world, ending up on the Grand Banks of Newfoundland in 1980. On February 14, 1982, a massive storm with winds up to ninety knots and waves measuring thirty metres (one hundred-feet) in height crashed into this "unsinkable" rig. Within twenty-four hours, it had disappeared from sight.

The Rooms Provincial Archives, A 41-36 (courtesy of Mobil Oil Canada Ltd., and G. & C. Associates)

Captain Doug Riley: "Gordie Barker was the biggest man in the pilots. At the time he retired he hit a peak of over four hundred pounds. When he hit that weight he was slow, but even when he was a hundred pounds overweight he was like Colin Wilson. He would climb up the ladder hand over hand. For a man his size it was unbelievable."

Beale—to get into the channel and out of the weather so I could board the pilot with safety. But this ship only did seven or eight knots and it was going to take the full day to get to Tahsis, so Colin was hoping to get on board there because, if that ship had had to go inside the buoy and we had to do the transfer there, it would be delayed about an hour and a half. They couldn't go in past Estevan Point during the hours of darkness, so he would have to stay offshore all night.

The ship was rocking back and forth, and the ladder was swinging out, then hitting the side, and we were up and down. Big swell. I said, "Jeez, Colin, I don't like it." He said, "I don't like it either, but I'll tell you what—if you can get alongside that ship, I can get the ladder." I knew his capabilities so I said, "Okay, but be careful." We went alongside, and he's trying to time it so that when we're on the top of a swell he can grab the ladder's highest point. But he doesn't catch the ladder until we're halfway down on the swell. I just grabbed the lever and went full astern. Then I looked to see where he was, and when I looked up, he's at the top of the ladder thumbing his nose at me. Getting him aboard off Cape Beale saved him that hour and a half, and they reached Tahsis just before dark.

Mickey Balatti always had a big smile on his face when he stepped on our boat. He only stood about five-foot-seven but he weighed about 230 pounds. He was very jovial and whenever he talked he had to tell you a story. In the sixties, before they had the radar monitoring for ships, Mickey was piloting on a freighter and approaching the First Narrows Bridge. A tug towing two barges was outbound. Whatever happened, the tug lost control of its barges, and they swung over toward Mickey Balatti's ship. He was at reduced speed so all he could do was go over far enough to avoid hitting the beach. As he went by, the two barges sideswiped him. There was no damage to the ship, but any time a pilot had an incident like that, he had to go and see the superintendent of the pilots and make out a report. Mickey had to wait in the office for his interview, and while he was waiting, he was telling some of his stories to the dispatchers, apparently not the least bit worried about the interview. When the secretary told him that he could go in, he said, "I'll be there in just a minute. I have one more story to tell."

A fellow by the name of Joe Higgs, who was well known throughout the tugboat industry and a great friend of mine, took over the storytelling after Mickey left. The first time I met him I told my wife that this guy was a character and that he just replaced

Mickey Balatti. All the foreign skippers particularly remembered him. I'm sure that if the Chinese skipper of a foreign-going ship, for instance, had Joe Higgs as a pilot, five years later when another pilot went up the ladder and was introduced to the captain, he would say, "How Captain Higg? He still well?" Such a popular man. Joe died last year.

My wife, Mickey, deckhanded on our boat for three or four years when things were a bit slow, and it brought a little more income into our family. One November she was on the boat with Fred Mathers, and they were going out to board pilot Walter Cullinen on a Polish freezer boat that was going in to Main Bay to stand by at anchor for four or five days while the Polish fleet brought in their catch and loaded it on the boat. While the weather wasn't pure fog, it was hazy and the visibility was limited to a mile or mile-and-a-half. They were going through a gap near Wizard Island and Fred said, "I see smoke. That's where I take my family in the summer. We built a lean-to there. Is somebody burning it down?" So he diverted and went through the other pass, and there's a man waving his arms. Fred put the lifeboat over and picked him up. The man's son and another boy were about a mile away on the other side of the island and the three of them had been there since the previous night. They had been on a small open boat that capsized. Fred called the Coast Guard, got the man warm, then went around to the other side and blasted the horn. All of a sudden the two young fellows came out from the bush. The boys' legs were all scraped and bruised from hitting against the rocks. The Coast Guard brought the lifeboat around and took them off and into Bamfield. They wouldn't have lasted another night. It was lucky that the fellow started burning because it was the smoke that caught Fred's attention.

Another time when I wasn't on the boat, Fred and Mickey were heading back home, going through one of the passes, and they saw a small yacht from Port Alberni just bobbing up and down in the water. They called out but there was no answer, so Fred jumped on board and here was the man and wife and children all passed out in the cabin from carbon monoxide. So they opened the doors, pulled them outside, and revived them. We are all required to have first aid training, which comes in handy in these emergency situations.

A retired pilot, Blackie Layton, told us a story about the GPS—which is a great invention if used properly. Blackie was on a cruise ship, a sixty-five- or seventy-thousand-tonner carrying about fifteen hundred people. They were in reduced visibility, maybe about half a

At the turn of the fifties, Mickey Balatti worked for Island Tug and Barge. He was entering the Strait of Juan de Fuca, and the company sent a tug out to relieve him of his barge and sent him out to pick up another one. He phoned his wife to say that he was going to be delayed another ten days. Now, for anyone working at a logging camp or on boats in those days the night's entertainment was to turn on the radio and listen to the telephone calls because they could hear both sides of the conversations. Mickey hadn't been home in three weeks. So he said to his wife in his high-pitched, squeaky voice, "You know, honey, if I don't get home pretty soon, I'm going to have to go out and buy something." Of course, the whole coast was listening, and she comes right back with, "If you don't send some money home soon, I'm going to have to go out and sell something."

mile, so he was going in at reduced speed when he got a contact on his radar. He checked it again after a couple of minutes and it was getting closer. He could tell from the radar that, if they both maintained their speed and course, there would be a collision. He finally got hold of the fellow on the boat through channel 16 and got him to switch to channel 6. It was just a small yacht, so Blackie told the yachtsman that the cruise ship had the right-of-way. According to regulations the oncoming vessel would have to give way. So the pilot said to him, "What are your intentions?" The guy answers back, "I'm just going to maintain my speed and course." So the pilot says, "But you're the giving vessel!" The yachtsman responded, "I can't change. I've got my GPS set while I'm going from point A to point B and I'm not at point B yet so I can't change course." So Blackie says, "Well, you may not have to worry about it."

A ship named the *Thorseggen* had topped off and finished loading its cargo at Gold River and was outbound for California. Normally we would go off Cape Beale for about two miles, and the pilot on that ship would come down the Jacob's ladder and we'd bring him back to Port Alberni. But it was the worst night I'd ever seen out there. Before my wife and I even got to the entrance we were going up and down with this heavy, heavy swell, about thirty-five feet high, and it was breaking right across from Seapool Buoy onto the beach. Whenever my boat went down, I'd lose complete sight of the ship. From that point out to one or two miles off Cape Beale, my sixty-five-foot boat, the *R.D. Riley,* would normally take about twenty minutes to reach that position, but with water like that I knew it would take an hour at least. I got the pilot on the radio and asked if they were going to bring the ship inside the channel but he told me that the captain didn't want to come inside. I said, "I don't think that there's a hope in hell that I can get you off." He told me to come out and have a look at it, which I did, but I couldn't see it happening. Then I saw the deck lights come on. The pilot radioed back that they agreed the water was too rough to disembark out there, but the captain was concerned that with such a big swell running and his draught of twenty-six feet, it would be dangerous for him to come in past Seapool Buoy in case he came down on a swell and touched bottom. So he decided to take the pilot right to California with him. Which he did.

We had got as far as Cape Beale and now I timed myself to turn around. The best way was to bring her up on top of the swell, and I cranked her hard over and brought her around. Now I had the

The *R.D. Riley*, formerly the *R.E. Riley*, was photographed here in 1976, is a twenty-metre (sixty-five-foot) pilot boat stationed in Port Alberni that has provided excellent service for many years.
Courtesy Captain D. Riley

following sea behind me so I opened up going in, and all of a sudden this one started to breach me. I started slipping sideways and I brought her right back. My wife screamed at me, "You run in slow!" If it had caught me, it would have just flipped me right over. Oh, she was scared. Normally when you get inside Seapool Buoy you can resume normal speed, but even two miles inside they were still running big. That was one of the last trips my wife took.

There is no more pilot boat service out of Port Alberni now. Helicopters and float planes transfer the pilots on and off ships. Also, there is a real decrease in shipping coming in there. Twenty years ago about eight or nine ships a month would come into the inlet to pick up or deliver cargo. Now there is one a month to pick up lumber. And where years ago there were two ships coming and going from there to California with paper and later it was barges, now it's trucks that take the paper products out of Port Alberni.

When Doug Riley retired in 2002, Lloyd McGill of Port Hardy bought the R.D. Riley *from him. Now, on contract to the Pacific Pilotage Authority, he transfers pilots to and from mainly cruise ships at Port Hardy.*

CHAPTER FOUR

Steampots to Dozers

Tugboats

"The deckhand had the engineer start up the engine, hook onto the tank and proceed out of False Creek, but he forgot to signal the bridge tender to open it. The tug went under the highest span but it wasn't high enough. When the mast hit the bridge, something had to give, and we were lucky it was the mast and not the wheelhouse. The mast broke off, but it didn't wake the skipper or me, even though it must have fallen onto the wheelhouse with a loud clatter."

Captain Harold Beck

In 1949, the US Army Tug *Major Richard M. Strong* ran aground off Vancouver Island and there seemed little chance of salvage. However, Straits Towing, Island Tug and Barge and Pacific Salvage pooled their resources and salvaged her in just fourteen days. Island Tug and Barge of Victoria acquired the thirty-six-metre (one-hundred-twenty-foot) tug after the rescue efforts, rebuilt her and renamed her the *Island Sovereign*. With a fourteen-hundred-horsepower engine, the *Island Sovereign* was considered one of the most powerful offshore tugs in the North Pacific.

Courtesy Seaspan International Ltd.

The towboating industry on the coast of British Columbia began with the Hudson's Bay Company's S.S. *Beaver*, a thirty-one-metre-long paddlewheeler with a pair of thirty-five-horsepower engines, which arrived here in 1835. Though the company intended it to be used to supply posts and collect furs, it quickly found its place towing

Downriver from the Patullo Bridge, an assist tug's deckhand attaches a tow line to a log boom. The main tug tows from the front of the boom while the assist tug helps keep the boom in line under the bridge.

Ed Whitebone photo

sailing ships into port. Later it was used to tow log booms and barges. Modifications to this original "steampot" established the basic design for all future tugboats on this coast—a high, forward-mounted pilot-house and a long, low afterdeck.

As the logging and lumbering industries grew over the next

century, so did the need for boats that could tow ocean-going ships as well as log booms and lumber barges, and in time a fleet of specialized tugboats came to be built. The design of BC's tugboats today incorporates some of the most advanced marine technology in the world, and they have become specialized to handle the berthing of ships, towing log booms and log barges, and wrangling barges full of wood chips, pulp, paper and other commodities—in general becoming the workhorses of this coast.

Captain Harold Beck, a long-time pilot, recalls his earlier days on the tugs.

In 1945, when I was nearly sixteen years old, I started as a deckhand on board the steamtug *Faultless* bound for Union Bay for bunkers. This was near the tail end of the "steampots." In those days when boats were taking on coal in Union Bay, the Chinese shore workers would be below deck, shovelling the coal into the side bunkers

This small river tug is towing a log boom to a mill on the Fraser River.
Ed Whitebone photo

Opposite: Loaded with 5,650 cubic metres (2,394,000 board feet) of cedar from Kelley Logging Co., this is thought to have been the largest Davis raft ever to pass under the Second Narrows Bridge. The steamtug *Ivanhoe* is towing the load to Port Moody.
Courtesy Harold Beck

Stevedores are unloading coal onto a dock in Vancouver Harbour in the early 1900s.
Vancouver Public Library, VPL 2930

located on both sides of the boiler. If there was too much coal coming down the chute, they would yell because the chute was made to load cargo ships, not tugs, so it could deliver more coal than they could handle in that cramped space. When I was in control of the amount of coal coming down, it was always a worry for me that I wouldn't hear them.

My first couple of days at the helm of the *Faultless* I was chasing the compass around, but after a while I became accustomed to steering by compass. We took on coal and headed north to Gowlland Harbour to pick up a thirty-six-section log boom and then tow it to Ladysmith. On our way back a westerly blew up. At the time, the gas boat was hanging in radial davits and was tied against the bulwarks, and the skipper ordered us to haul it to the boat deck. My soft hands were so sore from handling rusty boom chains that when I started pulling on the block and tackle rope, I could hardly hold onto it. I wasn't much use that night.

Captain Harold Beck: "One time on the steamtug *Dauntless*, when we got to Union Bay we were short of a coal passer—the guy who shovelled the coal inside the hull toward the firebox where the fireman was firing the boiler. The new fellow came from town all dressed in white—those were all the clothes he had—but they didn't stay white for long. Coal dust always went everywhere. To keep our accommodation clean, we had to wash it down regularly. Later when I was on diesel tugs, our clothes would smell of diesel. You weren't aware of it but when you went ashore your family soon told you about it."

The 122-tonne steam tug *Dauntless*, 28 metres (92 feet) long, was built in New Westminster and operated for many years for Pacific (Coyle) Navigation.
Vancouver Maritime Museum

On our second log tow from Gowlland Harbour to Ladysmith we ran into a strong southeast wind in Malaspina Strait just off Scotch Fir Point, which forced us into Jervis Inlet but not before it shook up our flat log boom. We lost a few logs, too. When we tied up in Agamemnon Channel we had to restore some of the boom. Being so new on this job, I didn't have a pair of caulk boots and there was a lot of work to repair the tow. Someone loaned me his old boots, which were way too large. I should have had three or four pairs of socks on to help fill out the boots. It took us two or three days to straighten out the boom, and by that time my feet were so sore I could hardly walk. I learned a couple of lessons there.

Around 1948 I was mate on the tug *Stormer* and we were towing an oil barge from Ioco into Pitt Lake and over to the Gulf Islands, delivering fuel oil to a few places along the way. We tied the oil barge to a buoy in English Bay and went into False Creek to pick up an oil tank for a logging camp at the head of Pitt Lake. The tank wasn't in the water when we arrived, so we all went to bed to wait till morning. My understanding was the tank was put into the water early in the morning, but the deckhand didn't call the skipper. Instead, he had the engineer start up the engine, hook onto the tank and proceed out of False Creek, but he forgot to signal the bridge tender to open it. The tug went under the highest span but it wasn't high enough. When the mast hit the bridge, something had to give, and we were lucky it was the mast and not the wheelhouse. The mast

The tugboat *Stormer* is seen here with a rebuilt mast after striking the bridge at False Creek.
Vancouver Maritime Museum 5173

broke off, but it didn't wake the skipper or me, even though it must have fallen onto the wheelhouse with a loud clatter. The deckhand and engineers nailed the mast up with two two-by-fours on either side of it. I woke up a short time later, found we were underway just west of Point Grey and took over the navigation. The skipper eventually got up and came into the wheelhouse. When he saw the two-by-fours holding the mast up, he looked at me. I looked at him. We didn't say anything. He found out later when he went down for a cup of coffee what had happened. I was amazed he hadn't waked up at the noise, as his room was just behind the wheelhouse.

In 1953 I went to Kingcome Navigation and joined the *J.S. Foley* towing Davis rafts out of the Queen Charlottes across to the mainland. In good weather, travelling at two knots, it took twenty-six hours-plus once you were in open waters. Usually we towed them

one at a time, but on one occasion we towed two rafts along the mainland coast with a one-and-a-quarter-inch wire from the bridles of the second raft right along the top of the logs of the first raft through to the tug's towline. When running the wire through the raft, you always made sure it was under the wires holding the raft together. On this trip south with two rafts, this top wire broke a few miles east of Cape Caution. By the time we got into Southgate and tied up the first raft, the other raft had hit one of the small islands east of Cape Caution and broke up because of the heavy swell conditions. There were logs all over the area. The company arranged for beach-combers to come in and salvage all that they could, and the company would pay them so much per log. But with the incoming tide and the westerly wind a lot of the logs came right into the Southgate area like they were corralled. The company, of course, wanted to reduce

Harold Beck was mate aboard the forty-metre (one-hundred-thirty-foot) steamtug *J.S. Foley*, operated by Kingcome Navigation.
Courtesy Harold Beck

Over the last century, the basic hull design hasn't changed much from that of the first wooden tugs, but there have been many substantial advances in tugboat technology. Following World War I, steam engines began to be replaced by diesel engines that were lighter, more compact and much more powerful. Here, the *S.D. Brooks*, formerly called *St. Faith*, is photographed in the late 1950s after her conversion to diesel fuel.

Courtesy Harold Beck

the price they were going pay the beachcombers, but what happened after that I don't know.

I got my 350-ton and tugboat master's ticket in 1953. That fall we moved a few rafts across Dixon Entrance and Hecate Strait from Masset and Cumshewa inlets to the mainland and tied them up in Chismore Pass or Captain Cove. Between the first week in November and Easter we didn't tow any rafts across Dixon Entrance or Hecate Strait because of southeasterly and northeasterly gales, although we were still working. The only break we had in December was four or five days off when we steamed south to Vancouver for Christmas, but they sent us back up to the Charlottes again before the New Year. It snowed and blew northerly. Every morning the deck was covered with snow up to the bulwarks. It kept us shovelling.

On our trip out on Easter Sunday we had to let the log raft go six miles off Triple Island in a northeasterly that came up with one big bang. I was off watch and sleeping when the captain sent the deckhand to my cabin to tell me to let the towline go. When I arrived at the towing winch, the tow cable was over the starboard quarter and the main engine was stopped. I opened up the brake on the towing winch but the cable didn't pull free, and the deckhand and I had to unbolt the gearbox cover to get at the clamp to free the towline. It was a terrible job because the wind was freezing cold and the tug was churning around on the swells. The captain didn't want to put power onto the propeller because the towline could have gotten caught up in it. The only parts of the raft we recovered were the sidesticks, all the wires and the tug's towline off Rose Spit. The *S.D. Brooks* came up from Cumshewa to help us tow the sticks and wires over to Chismore Pass on the mainland side. The *Brooks* power-buckled the sidestick wires onto another raft and we recovered our towline.

In 1954 I was given my first skipper's job on the *R. Bell-Irving*, and the next year instead of booms we began to use log barges, the *Powell 1* and *Powell 2*. Although they were still building Davis rafts

By the mid-fifties most Davis rafts had been replaced by log barges such as the *Powell No 1*. Vancouver Maritime Museum 3782

Photographed in 1958, the 45-metre (148-foot) tug *N.R. Lang*, owned by Kingcome Navigation, is one of the last tugs to have towed a Davis raft. By the mid-fifties most rafts had been replaced by log barges.

Courtesy Harold Beck

until 1958, most of the time I was towing log barges after that. On the *N.R. Lang* I brought the last of the rafts across from the Charlottes for Kingcome and the last three Davis rafts south from Captain Cove to Teakerne Arm. There was fine weather along the whole coast so I thought it would be an easy ten to eleven days tow, but we got caught up in a moderate swell and westerly wind in Queen Charlotte Sound and were losing a few cedar logs off the front of the first raft. The other two rafts were hemlock and were okay. I had to go into Smith Inlet and anchor to wait for the weather to moderate and tighten up some wires on the cedar raft. I didn't have enough swinging room in the bay for three rafts, so I had to fold the one raft against the other.

On another trip to Masset with a log barge in tow, while entering Principe Channel, I received a call from our office asking me if could help the tug *Commodore Straits* that was adrift off Dundas Island at Dixon Entrance. They had lost their log barge and the tug's rudder. The first job I had to do was to take our own log barge to a safe anchorage. The best place would be Captain Cove, and after anchoring it, we headed for Dixon Entrance and arrived at the stricken Straits tug in the early morning, but he wouldn't take our towline because he was waiting for a sister tug. A southeast gale was still blowing on the north coast, but the weather was good enough that he wouldn't be in trouble for a few hours.

Their office came on the radio then and asked me to go look for the barge, the *Forest Prince.* I told them I would have to clear it with our office, which I did. Then I went on the radio and called the skipper on the *Commodore* and asked him to give me their position

The tug *Commodore Straits* heads out of Vancouver after fuelling up in Coal Harbour. Built in 1920, it was the last active seagoing steamtug on the BC coast.
Ed Whitebone photo

when they lost the barge. We steamed to that position and set a course that would take us to Cape Chacon on Prince of Wales Island. The surf was that was hitting the rocks and shoreline was spraying fifty feet into the air. Four of us were on the bridge with binoculars looking for the log barge or its remains while we steamed north along the east coast of the island. Still not sighting it, we cut across the channel to Gravina Island and steamed south, still looking. That's when an aircraft came on the radio and told us that we had just gone by the small cove where the barge was stranded. So we turned around and went back to the entrance, but you couldn't see the barge from there because the cove was L-shaped. We steamed into it with the depth sounder on, checking the depth of water under the keel, and spotted the barge on the beach at the far end of the cove. We were amazed that it had gotten through the cove entrance. A bit of southwest wind must have come up and pushed it. That barge must have had a charmed life as this wasn't its first stranding.

After anchoring, we used one of our lifeboats to go and check the barge for damage, but my crew weren't watching the ebb tide and the lifeboat went aground. We put the other boat in the water to bring the crew back for lunch. Afterwards, we ran a wire rope from the barge to the tug to be ready for a high water tow plus the recovery of the grounded lifeboat. Finally, about six o'clock that evening we started pulling the barge off the beach. It came off quite easily because it was one of the larger high tides. After coupling the towline onto the barge we headed for Prince Rupert, stopping off at Annette Island to sound the barge's tanks as it was taking on a slight list. The odd tank had water in it but nothing to worry about.

The next time I was on the *S.D. Brooks* we were about halfway between Browning Entrance and Rose Spit, heading for Masset Inlet, at about seven in the morning when Bill Dalmage, the manager, telephoned. He usually never phoned, leaving that job up to the dispatcher. His new orders were to take our barge to Alfred Bay in Skidegate Inlet. So we set our course for there. It had been blowing a gale during the previous night, and off Jedway we heard someone calling on the radio, "Who's going to come and save me?" The caller was on a small tug and couldn't start its engine but he had two empty barges and an oil barge in tow. Finally a fisherman towed him in to shore but left the barges floating free in Hecate Strait. I heard that Straits Towing were going to send a tug for them from Kitimat, but after I tied our barge up in Alfred Bay, I asked the office if we could go out and try to find the abandoned barges. We came out of

The tug *Commodore Straits* is in dry dock at the Allied Shipbuilders shipyard, located at the mouth of the Seymour River on the North Shore of Vancouver Harbour.

Ed Whitebone photo

Bob Acreman was a tugboat skipper and master for nearly twenty-nine years. He is a direct descendant of John Muir, the first white settler in Sooke, BC.

Courtesy Bob Acreman

Skidegate again, set up an intercept course, and found them about two o'clock in the morning. We picked up the full barge first because they were running out of oil at Jedway, then we picked up the other two barges and arrived there at slow speed. Later I spoke to the company about salvage, and the tug's crew finally did get some extra money for both salvage jobs.

One day we came into Vancouver Harbour at Moodyville, now Neptune Terminals, and while we were dumping the logs off the barge, the towline's bit sank to the sea floor. When we heaved the towline in, we found an old sailing ship's anchor attached to it. We had the anchor against the bulwarks, then we put another wire on it to get the towline free. I was standing at the after controls, and my crewman was standing on the poop deck near the wire when it broke. It went right over his head, hardly missing him. It could have killed him. That was the last we saw of the historic anchor.

Captain Bob Acreman was born in 1935 and is the only direct descendant still living in Sooke of the first white settlers there, the Muirs. John Muir, Captain Bob's great-great-grandfather pre-empted land in Sooke in 1852. Bob worked on tugs from the age of twenty-one until he retired on July 27, 1997, at age sixty-two.

Mother always bragged to everybody that I could row a boat when I was five. I rowed all over the harbour. My step-grandfather, a great fisherman, taught me fishing. In 1953 after I finished high school, I went to work at the fish traps but then decided that I would try to get a job on a tugboat because that's where two of my buddies worked. I started on tugs in January 1956, moved to Island Tug and Barge, then to Seaspan, receiving my Masters Certificate in 1967.

I started on the *Island Champion,* and it became the escort vessel for Marilyn Bell when she swam from Port Angeles to Victoria. We were there for her first attempt, the one that failed, and were also with her on her successful swim.

On New Years Eve 1961 we were laying to on the *Island Challenger* in Port Renfrew, getting ready to celebrate the New Year, when a shotgun "bang" went flying around the government dock. It was Murray Smith, the foreman for the BC Forest Products' booming ground operation up there. I recall him saying, "You'd better phone your office," which Captain [Andrew] Mickey MacPherson did. It turned out there was a Greek freighter, the *Glafkos,* on the beach off Amphitrite Point near Ucluelet on the north side of Barkley Sound.

We got up there in the middle of the night and it was hopeless. The wind was so bad we couldn't do anything. Very heavy seas. To this day they're the biggest seas I ever saw in my life. So we just ran in and hid in Ucluelet until daylight, and then went out again. By this time the old steamtug *Sudbury* was out there with the Greek freighter, and we somehow managed to get a line on the freighter. Took us pretty much all day, but we were able to maintain a strain on the line and keep it off the rocks. The next morning our engine started to fail so we

In February 1968, the *Island Sovereign* was one of three tugs that assisted the *Suwaharu Maru* after it collided with the *Mandoil II*. The weather was fierce on the night of the rescue but conditions eventually calmed down enough for the tugs to attach lines and tow the ship to Nootka Sound.

Courtesy Seaspan International Ltd.

On New Year's Eve in 1961, a Greek freighter heading for the Juan de Fuca Strait hit the rocks near Esperanza Inlet. All hands disembarked safely but tugboats were unable to reach the freighter, and after sitting on the beach for about a week, it broke up in a storm. One can still see part of the bow on the beach.
Courtesy Captain Ozzie Nilssen

somehow or other had to get the line over to the *Sudbury*, which we did. What a mighty old thing she was. A towboat at its highest.

We went into Ucluelet and the engineers got our engine patched up. We got out there again just about the time the anchor chains on the Greek freighter broke, so we got a line on to help with the tow. Of course, this was getting fairly late in the evening. The next morning, after towing all night, we arrived in Esquimalt. I tell you, I was never so glad to see dry land in my life. I told myself that, if I ever get out of these carryings-on, I'm never going to sea again—ever. That feeling lasted about a day-and-a-half. We then headed back to

Victoria. I think we had a day off, but the next day we were headed back to Port Renfrew to start from square one again.

In February 1968 a Japanese freighter, the *Suwaharu Maru,* hit a Liberian tanker, the *Mandoil II,* right in the centre of the starboard side. There was an immediate explosion. A lot of the Greek seamen lost their lives because the ship pretty much burned itself out with the exception of the centre castle which was a midships housework. We went out on the *Island Monarch.* The weather was terrible. *Sudbury II* was already out there and did get a line on the ship but it broke, so we had to wait a couple of days until the weather calmed down and the *Island Sovereign* showed up. Then both the *Sovereign* and the *Sudbury II* got lines on the ship. Our old *Island Monarch,* a kind of a gutless wonder, just went along for the ride. It took about three days to get this thing the six hundred miles back into Nootka Sound. It still had a lot of cargo on it, oil that is called Sumatra crude. Apparently in Indonesia this stuff goes right out of the ground and into their cars. Volatile. You hold a glassful of it up and it looks like diesel oil. When it was time to check out the ship's tanks for the amount of gas vapours in them, it took about three puffs to get the meter up to ninety—really fast. Garbage was a problem out there, so I sent some guys onto the shore with a bunch of garbage to see if they could burn it. The fire was slow in catching, so when the tide was down, I gave them a paint can full of Sumatra crude. They threw that on and it just went POOF!—black smoke and a flash of red. That was the end of it. No fire at all. The *Mandoil II* stayed up there until August when it was towed to Esquimalt.

I was mate on the *Island Navigator* with John Webb as master. We were going into Seattle in heavy fog, and I was sound asleep when there was a bone-jarring crash. I jumped out of bed just in time to watch the *Hyak,* one of Washington state's superferries, going down the side of us. It did an awful pile of damage to our tug and hit our railway barge tow so hard that when the towline came tight it shot the barge backwards. The line hit one of the pins we have for keeping the towline in place and shot it about two hundred feet up in the air. The barge hit the overhang on the ferry's starboard car deck and demolished it, and then the barge shot out backwards from underneath the cars. The centre and portside strings of cars came forward and the front ones lost their front wheels. As I recall, that was the only time that I was ever involved in a collision.

In the summer of 1970 Island Tug and Vancouver Tug and Barge amalgamated and formed Seaspan International. Of course the boats

During the night of Sunday, December 31, 1961, amid gale-force winds and twenty-foot seas the *Glafkos,* a 7,000-tonne, 440-foot-long Greek freighter on its way from Japan to Vancouver, struck an island off Amphitrite Point at low tide. The hull was spiked on a rock pinnacle, and the engine room and two of the ship's five holds were flooded. On Tuesday, January 2, the salvage tugs *Sudbury* and *Island Challenger* managed to get a towline aboard after two attempts and for the next twenty-four hours held the ship off the rocks just seven hundred yards away. They had hoped to pull it off the shore at high tide, but when the ship struck, the captain had ordered the anchors out and, without power, they could not be hauled up again. It was only when the seas subsided somewhat that the *Sudbury* was able to transfer cutting equipment aboard, the anchors were cut away, and the long tow to Esquimalt could begin. In the meantime an RCAF helicopter had taken most of the thirty-man crew to safety, leaving only the captain and a skeleton crew aboard.

On the night of February 28, 1968, in dense fog 340 miles off the mouth of the Columbia River, the 8,780-ton Japanese freighter *Suwaharu Maru*, carrying lumber from Coos Bay, Oregon, to Japan, rammed the 24,502-tonne Liberian tanker *Mandoil II*, carrying 300,000 barrels of Sumatra light crude oil from Manila to Tacoma, Washington. There was an immediate explosion and both ships were set afire. After the groundswell worked the ships apart, they drifted helplessly in the fog. However, the freighter's "Mayday" message had been heard by the nearby freighter *Kure Maru*, which picked up thirty-two of the *Mandoil II*'s Greek crew from lifeboats; eleven crew members were missing and presumed to have died in the explosion and fire. An American tanker took the thirty-seven Japanese crewmen from the deck of the burning *Suwaharu Maru*.

all had their names changed to Seaspan whatever. Originally there was a lot of ill feeling among the people but it all smoothed over. They were actually a pretty good bunch to work for. In fact, I found out in June 1992, when my wife and I lost our son, that no one could be better treated than we were. I was skipper on pretty much everything they had.

In 1977 when things were getting slow in the Victoria industry, I applied to Seaspan in Vancouver and was posted as master of the *Seaspan Warrior*, beloved old thing. I spent the next seven years as master of that vessel. She was a fantastic seaboat, pulled very well. Really quite comfortable. While on the *Warrior* I spent one day, January 8, 1978, that I'll never forget. Skippers have to be ready to deal with anything at a moment's notice, but this situation was far beyond anything I'd ever had to deal with before. We were bound from Vancouver to Seattle and were just passing the ferry terminal at Tsawassen at 11:30 a.m.. George Karn was the seaman on my watch, and he went below to call the seaman for the next watch. In a few minutes George came running back to the wheelhouse and told me that I'd better go and see this fellow because he was cold, didn't move and wouldn't wake up. I went and looked and he was very dead. So we notified the Canada Coast Guard. They arrived by hovercraft, accompanied by an RCMP officer, and took the poor fellow away while we headed back to Vancouver. On arrival we got descended upon by every imaginable authority. You would not believe some of the questions we were asked, right down to wondering if our cook had poisoned him. It turned out that he had died of an epileptic

The deep-sea tug *Sudbury II* stands by the Liberian tanker *Mandoil II* after its collision with a Japanese freighter in February 1968, which left a twenty-seven-metre (ninety-foot) gash in its starboard bow.
Courtesy Adrian Bull

seizure. He had kept it so quiet that his wife didn't even know that he had epilepsy.

I worked with some wonderful people over the years. There were some, of course, you didn't get along with but you had to respect their professionalism. A fellow asked me the day I retired, "Bob, what's the thing that you're most proud of?" I was dumbfounded. I'd never really done anything heroic, so I had to think about it for a few minutes. I said, "You know, I think the thing that I'm most proud of is the fact that I, with the throttles, never hurt anybody." I like to

The *Seaspan Warrior* is a gas tug built in 1959. It has had several name changes, including *Seaspan Warrior* in 1971 and *Sea Warrior* in 2002. Captain Bob Acreman fondly remembers the *Seaspan Warrior* as a "beloved, comfortable old thing."
Courtesy Seaspan International Ltd.

Captain Bob Acreman: "The cook is a very important person on board. One of the best I had with me was old Gordie Gordienko who used to be a professional wrestler. Great guy, great cook. Cooks didn't really have a steady boat and Gordie spent a lot of time on the bigger boats, but then his legs started to act up and he couldn't handle the heavy weather. Gordie was with me on and off for a long time, and I was glad to have him. He could make anything. Nobody could cook a prime rib of beef like him. I'm three-quarters cannibal when it comes to that sort of thing."

The *Seaspan Rival*, built in 1968, is a steel tug that measures 11.28 metres (37 feet) in length.
Courtesy Seaspan International Ltd

think I survived twenty-eight-and-a-half years as skipper virtually trouble-free.

Captain Rick Stanley, currently a pilot, started early on tugs.

One day in the 1970s while I was decking on the *Seaspan Rival* with Jim Davies, we were heading up to Mission towing a couple of empty chippers. On the way up, we were miles from any houses when Jim saw a little rowboat sitting on the beach. He wanted to look at it so on the way back down we stopped. He couldn't get the tug in close to the beach. We moved some log booms and still couldn't reach it. So he decided to cross the booms to the shore, tried to run on water and fell in. This was January so the water was really cold. He was soaked but ran down the beach to the rowboat and found that there was no bottom in it. Now he couldn't get back out to the log booms, so he had to swim to the boat. He almost had hypothermia, poor guy. All for nothing. We were into more pranks when we were on the tugs. Those times were more relaxed and we were always into shenanigans. It was a lot of fun.

In 1982 I decided to go to the Arctic with Arctic Transportation Ltd. (ATL) and spent three years there as master on the *Arctic Ignik* and the *Arctic Kapvik*, two shallow-draft "ro-ro" [roll-on, roll-off] vessels. The Arctic equipment was larger than the regular tugs so I upgraded my ticket to Ocean Navigator One endorsement.

In the Arctic, no matter the cost, you do whatever you have to do to make it work. I remember I was going up the Mackenzie River and there was just not enough water for our boat. The Shotell jet is a 360-degree drive system that sucks the water from underneath and pushes it out, and consequently in shallow water she sucks up rocks from the bottom. I called the office to tell them this, and they told me that the system was supposed to run on wet grass and to just keep her going. I did more damage to the bloody props on this thing trying to get through the rapids, but that's what the boss wanted. I enjoyed the Arctic, but I wouldn't want to go back. It was a different way of life, and how we worked was totally different, twenty-four hours of daylight and different standards.

The *Seaspan Rustler* tows a loaded chip barge out from the tie-up on Sea Island near Richmond. Barges are filled with wood chips from sawmills up the Fraser River and are stored on Sea Island before being towed to coastal pulp mills such as Powell River and Port Mellon.
Ed Whitebone photo

I got involved in a salvage operation up there after one of the
vessels ran over a wellhead that punched a hole in her and she sank.
They were worried about pollution and they started a salvage operation with the Canadian Coast Guard's involvement. ATL had a great
big portable dry dock, and the tug *Arctic Hooper* was going to do the
job. I was running a large ro-ro vessel, a landing craft about 150 feet
long with a 45-foot beam. We had a great big heavy ramp on the
front and were going to assist the *Arctic Hooper* in moving the overturned vessel into the dry dock, which it wasn't designed for, but they
had anchored the dry dock facing the wrong way so that coming in
we had to go with the current, and of course that made the job a lot
more difficult. We couldn't get the derelict in. The current was too

The *Arctic Ignik*, a shallow draft ro-ro vessel with
a ramp that allows wheeled cargo to be driven
on and off easily, is docked at Tuktoyaktuk, NWT.
Courtesy Rick Stanley

strong. The skipper tried once but no luck. I tried to tell him that we couldn't do it because of the current, and he kept saying that we could. He kept putting more power to it, and by now our engine was going so fast I could see our ramp going right through the dry dock. I kept telling him to back out. Finally he did. Some Coast Guard were on our vessel too, and they shut our operation down. I told them if they had the dry dock turned around, we could get in with no trouble. So ATL had to take all of the anchors up, turn the dry dock around, let it find the current and set the anchors again. Then we got right in, no trouble.

We've lost some of the good places we used to go, like into Utah Mines in Quatsino Narrows. There's a lot of current in the area so you had to wait for high water slack to go in. It's a big turn to go in there, ninety degrees inside the narrows. It was really tight and you had to pay attention. Now the mine is closed. The same with the pulp mill on Watson Island. That's shut down now. But all of these experiences prepared me for my job as a pilot. I enjoyed the challenge.

When a sawmill requires logs, it contacts a towboat company that then opens the main boom and pulls aside the log sections that the mill has requested. Seen here on the North Arm of the Fraser River, a deckhand prepares to hook the tug's towline to a section of log boom that has just been cut loose from the main holding area.

Ed Whitebone photo

Captain Royal Maynard charting his course,
February 2003.

Courtesy Captain Royal Maynard

Captain Royal Maynard has worked on tugs since 1960 when he was seventeen. He received his master's ticket in 1966. He has skippered the Rivtow Capt. Bob, *the most powerful tug on the BC coast, for nine years. He lives with his wife, June, in Garden Bay on the Sunshine Coast, and they enjoy frequent trips up the coast on his sixty-six-foot boat, the* Universe, *a former seiner.*

On May 8, 2003, I was skipper on the *Rivtow Capt. Bob* with a crew of seven and four loaders for the barge. We were loading the log barge *Rivtow Hercules* in Nesook Bay out in Nootka Sound, an isolated location. The barge is 400 feet long with a 94-foot beam and carries a load of 15,000 tons of logs. We had about half of the load on and I had gone to bed, and around four o'clock in the afternoon the mate came and woke me up and told me that there was a fire on the forward crane on the barge. I didn't realize the seriousness of the fire until I had a look, and then I was aware that there was a significant problem out there. My first thought was for the crane operator. Where was he? I was relieved to hear that he had gotten out okay by climbing down the series of steps and ladders inside the crane tower. No one else was on the barge.

The mate wanted to go up there to try to put the fire out, but it was too dangerous. It was a pretty hot and dangerous fire, with molten aluminum dropping from the crane and great plumes of black smoke and flames shooting out of every opening. When the fire became really hot, I moved the tug away from the barge, letting out a couple of hundred feet of line, as we were afraid of a possible explosion up in the crane that could do damage to the tug or someone aboard. Our next move was to try and get some water onto the load itself so that the logs didn't catch on fire. We got one of the forest company's helicopters to come in with a bucket and start dropping water on the fire, which would cool things off but it couldn't penetrate into the cab itself. We also made arrangements for one of the Martin Mars water bombers to come in from Sproat Lake because they carried much more water than the helicopters. By now flames were shooting out to the crane's cabin, but the water bomber didn't arrive for nearly two hours. These planes carry 7,200 gallons of water—60,000 pounds—per drop. He made four drops then had to leave because it was starting to get dark. We lay there overnight. The maintenance people from our company arrived by plane, and just before dawn they went up into the tower and looked around. We

rigged several fire hoses together so they could take them up with them to cool things off.

The fire had gotten hot enough to melt everything in the crane that was meltable, including the inch-and-five-eighths cable used as a topping line, and it dropped the crane's boom onto the load of logs, which effectively wrecked the boom. The next morning we got away from Nesook Bay and went into Vancouver Harbour, arriving on the afternoon of April 10, tying up the barge at one of the anchorages. The company brought a crane barge out and removed the broken boom and the grapple from the top of the load. Two or three days later we moved the barge out to Andy's Bay in Howe Sound, which is where the load was originally destined to be unloaded. They had to load a bunch more wood on the barge with the back crane to give it enough height and weight to be able to dump properly, as it was a

The *Rivtow Capt. Bob* returns from a trip up north, having dropped off an empty self-dumping log barge that had been unloaded in Howe Sound.
Ed Whitebone photo

self-loading, self-dumping barge. While the loaders were doing that, we went down to Langdale to pick up the *Queen of Surrey* ferry, which had also had a serious fire, and towed it up to Deas Basin terminal. Then we ran out and dumped the logs off of our barge and took it to Vancouver again. It was an interesting day. The company removed a bunch more stuff out of the crane and about a week and a half later we towed the barge over to the graving dock in Esquimalt. They have a 150-ton crane there that lifted the cab of our crane off the top of the tower and set it down on the deck. We then towed it back to Vancouver and the company went to work rebuilding it. The head loader, who was on the crane when the fire started, was involved as well as our own maintenance people and various other companies. I gather that it was a very expensive fire. The barge, which is the company's biggest, was out of commission from the day of the fire, May 8, until we did our first commercial trip on October 2.

About three years ago a killer whale started showing up in Nootka Sound when we'd be loading. It would come right into the loading area with us, pushing bundle booms and dozer boats around. He's now called Luna, and he's very friendly to humans, which is not a good thing. The serious situation is that he's done damage to fish-boats, sailboats, floatplanes and small boats. The Fisheries were going to move him out of there, but the First Nations people in the area felt that the whale was a reincarnation of their chief who died about the same time that the whale showed up there. So every time that the crew that was going to remove the whale showed up to catch him, the First Nations people would lure him away, so he is still out there now. He's getting to be quite large. I heard a story about a couple of fellows that were out there fishing in a small boat and he came right under the boat, lifted it out of the water and dropped it back in again.

I don't know what the final outcome for that whale is going to be. He's quite a nuisance now when we're trying to load logs. On one assignment we were going in to Nootka Sound with an empty barge, making about ten knots—about eleven and a half miles per hour—and that whale stayed right alongside of us, about thirty feet off the side of the tug, all the way in there for about twelve miles at that speed. Never slowed down a bit. We saw him out there one day with a broken boomstick. This was about a thirty-foot log a foot-and-a-half in diameter. He had his mouth on one end of it and was pushing it along in the water. He does the same thing with small tugboats and

dozer boats, the one-man assist boats. One skipper on a forty-foot tug refers to him as his bow thruster. He's a powerful animal. I often wonder when we're pulling the barge if he's going to get too close to the nozzle and get sucked into the propeller. From the scars on him he's obviously been hit by propellers. [Unfortunately, Royal's prediction came true. On March 10, 2006, Luna was sucked into the propeller of a thirty-metre tug in Nootka Sound.]

In about 1969 I was on the tug *M.R. Cliff* in Halkett Bay in Howe Sound, tied up there because of a very strong and cold Squamish wind. Wherever the waves were breaking against the shore, the rocks were covered with ice. There was a troller-type fishboat, about forty-two feet long, running across to Horseshoe Bay when his fuel line broke and dumped all of his fuel into the bilge. Luckily it was diesel because that doesn't explode like gas. His engine quit, but

L98, or Luna as he was called by the public, arrived in Nootka Sound in 2001. Killer whales are very social animals, and separated from his pod, Luna attempted to befriend passing boats and seaplanes. The situation ended in tragedy when he was killed by the propeller of tug *General Jackson*, March 10, 2006.
Courtesy Lance Barrett-Lennard

The old wooden tugboat *M.R. Cliff* was named for its original owner.

Vancouver Maritime Museum 19423

he couldn't get below to see what he could do because it was blowing between sixty and seventy knots. We were on our way over to Long Bay to help another tug that was doing some yarding and needed help to hold the booms when I got a call from the old ferry, the *Sunshine Coast Queen,* that was on the Horseshoe Bay–Langdale run at that time. We turned around and went back to the fishboat. He had an anchor out but every time the bow lifted in the swell the anchor dragged a bit so now he was about thirty feet from the beach with at least a ten-foot sea running. We got a line on him and dragged him out to Halkett Bay. As far as I'm concerned, we saved the lives of the two fellows on board because they never would have made it if the boat had been smashed on the rocks under those conditions. We later towed them over to Gibsons where they could get more fuel.

A few years ago I saw a video about the *Rivtow Capt. Bob,* and at its end there was a short section showing a model of the boat running by remote control on Canim Lake. After some investigation, I found that this model was for sale by John Kobanuk, the man who built it. He had worked for CN on the tugs when he was young, then in 1950 got a gillnetter and for the next twenty-eight years was a commercial fisherman. He later went back on the tugs for Calley Towing for about a year. He and his wife, Jean, then moved to Canim Lake where he worked in a mine, finally retiring in 1983. It was after his retirement that he started building models of boats.

I contacted John by phone and a few weeks later my wife and I drove up to Canim Lake, met John and Jean, and bought the model of the *Rivtow Capt. Bob,* a beautiful piece of work. During a very pleasant visit with them we discovered that he had five other models

Captain Royal Maynard: "A friend of mine has a large vessel over two hundred feet long that he kept up at the Rainor Group in Queen Charlotte Straits for a summer getaway. His half-brother was caretaking the boat there and sprucing it up, and one morning about three years ago he went out in a small boat to check on some crab traps near where the ship was anchored, and he noticed that the buoy on one of his crab traps was moving across the bay. He managed to get hold of the buoy and pulled the trap up. There was a large halibut hooked up on it. He towed it back to the float, got the thing out of the water and onto the float and killed it with a sledge hammer. According to the length-to-weight measurement, which fishermen claim is very accurate, it would have weighed between 270 and 280 pounds—a very large halibut. As it happened, I was going by on the *Capt. Bob* and heard this fellow on the radio. Apparently, this halibut had been previously caught on commercial gear and had broken the leader. It had then gone after the crabs in the trap and had gotten hung up on the trap itself by this hunk of fish line coming out of its mouth. I guess it had been towing the trap around all night so it was pretty worn out when the half-brother got it. I assume that he was eating halibut for quite a while afterwards."

that he had built, and a couple of years later my wife purchased the model of the *M.R. Cliff* from him and gave it to me for my birthday. This meant a lot to me as I was master on her for her last commercial voyage as a tug. Last fall John made me a gift of a model of the *Moresby*, an old steam tug that was retired many years ago. These models are all approximately four feet in length and are very intricate in detail, very fine workmanship by a very fine and interesting man. I am proud to have them as part of my maritime collection.

Captain Royal Maynard displays his tugboat models at his home in Garden Bay, BC.
Courtesy Captain Royal Maynard

CHAPTER FIVE

Bubbleheads and Urchins

Dive Fishermen

"When he tried to climb into the boat, the octopus grabbed onto the hull and then grabbed his helmet and started tearing it off. He could feel the tentacles going up under his mask and along the side of his face . . . . Scared the living daylights out of him."

Steve "Sonny" Dennis, Diver

Wes Sampson tops off the sea urchin bag with the last of his harvest and the full bag is ready to be taken to the surface.

David McRae photo

The first commercial dive fishery in BC waters began in the early 1950s when scuba divers went down after abalone. By the 1970s there were nearly eighty divers at work harvesting up to 433 tonnes annually, but it took a mere twenty years for them to reduce abalone numbers so drastically that the fishery had to be closed. It is now illegal for either commercial or recreational fishers to take abalone.

Until the late nineteenth century, sea urchin populations on this coast had been kept in check by sea otters, but when these animals were almost wiped out for their furs, the urchin population surged. As a result, they decimated this coast's beds of kelp, their preferred food, and threatened other species that relied on the kelp. In the meantime a strong demand had developed for urchin roe for Japanese sushi, jump-starting a west coast fishery for red sea urchin; by the end of the 1970s there was also a fishery for the smaller green urchin. "The legal size limit for the reds was six-and-a-half inches," explains Dave Sweeney, who dived for them in the late 1980s. "If an urchin is healthy and getting lots of kelp to eat, it produces a nice yellow, almost a banana-yellow, roe, very fine, finer than salmon roe. From when we picked the product to the time it hit the Asian market, it took about forty-eight hours. The shell is worth nothing, except dried as an ornament." The red urchin fishery peaked in 1992—a year before quotas were established—with about 13,000 tonnes delivered by 291 divers; the green urchin fishery peaked the same year with

For those who have acquired the taste, red sea urchin roe is much finer than salmon roe.
David McRae photo

Geoduck harvesters use blasts of high-pressure water to uncover these burrowing clams in the sandy seabed.
Rick Harbo photo

1,042 tonnes collected by 191 divers. "There are still a lot of urchin divers around," says Dave Sweeney, "but the licences are getting scarcer."

The commercial harvest of geoducks began in the late 1970s. The diver grasps the exposed siphon of this enormous clam and, using a jet of high-pressure water, loosens the sand or mud surrounding the clam's body. "Geoduck shells don't come together like regular clams," explains Sonny Dennis, one of the pioneers of the BC dive fishery. "There are hinges on the back and a soft, kind of leathery skin called the mantle that comes up the front, and the siphon comes out of that. Both the body meat and the siphon are used—only the guts are discarded. The biggest geoduck was dug out off Ucluelet—twenty-six pounds." As a result of the intensive dive fishery in recent years, geoducks are now scarce in intertidal waters and are mainly found at depths of 20–30 metres, although some are as deep as 120 metres. In the early days of this fishery there was no quota, but today there are fifty licences allotted, each for about twenty-six tonnes. Although Japan was the original market for BC geoducks, most are now shipped live to mainland China and Hong Kong.

Back around 1980 Sonny Dennis was also one of the first on this coast to commercially harvest California sea cucumbers, which grow up to sixteen inches in length and are destined mainly for the Chinese market. "They have a small amount of meat on the inside wall and the processors split them open and scrape off this meat. They also salt and dry the skin, I believe, and the Chinese use it as a kidney medicine."

In addition, there are commercial dive fisheries for scallops, horse clams and octopus in BC waters.

Steve (Sonny) Dennis, who owns Duffin Cove Resort in Tofino, is one of the "old-timers" of British Columbia's dive industry. He was still a teenager in 1979 when he and a friend earned their basic scuba tickets, bought dry suits and began diving throughout the winter, gathering abalone and other shellfish. The following year he began a seventeen-year career of commercial diving, logging approximately fifteen thousand hours underwater.

Once the meat has been removed, sea cucumber skins are salted and dried and then sold as kidney medicine.

Rick Harbo photo

When I started diving commercially, we would go down wearing up to 120 pounds of lead on our backs. We used a "hookah"—a surface-supply air line about 250 feet long—and carried about 250 feet of fire hose with around sixty pounds per square inch of water pressure coming out of the end of it to wash the sand from around the geoducks we were digging. It was a gorgeous sandy bottom with sea pens waving in the current, sun shining down through the water. We were walking around on the bottom like men on the moon.

An "old-timer" of the commercial dive industry, Steve Dennis began diving for geoducks as a young teenager. In his first few seasons he was making twenty-five hundred dollars a week.
Courtesy Steve Dennis

I was pretty excited and apprehensive at the same time, but my friend had some experience and he made the digging look so easy. It took him five or six seconds to dig one geoduck, then he handed me the stinger, the end of the water hose that right-angles down to the bottom. It took five or ten minutes for me to dig one, while he sat patiently and watched me. The siphon and the body—where the shell is—can be just a few inches under the sand or four to five feet underneath, and I dug this massive hole big enough for me, doing a lot of extra work and then climbed in. I got my hand on the end of the siphon that extends upwards from the body—the shell and the

Once his mask is tightened and his harvest bag is attached to his hip, Steve Dennis is ready for a descent.

Courtesy Steve Dennis

siphon together can be up to four feet in length—but as you grab the snout and start digging, they pull you down and down. All the time I was digging I couldn't see a thing with all of the sand in the water. My legs were floating way up over my head, then my lead weights fell off, and my friend was trying to hold me and the hose down and put my weights back on all at the same time. When I finally got this thing out, I put it on the bottom to look at it, quite proud of myself. My friend stuck it in his bag. I finally got my second one and he put that one in his bag too. I thought, oh no, no more. And I went up to the boat and got my own water hose and went down again to dig. That first day I dug sixteen geoducks and I think he dug close to six hundred.

The problem I had as a new diver was that I couldn't see the tips of the siphons in the sand at all. My friend could see them everywhere, and he showed me the little indents in the sand but I still couldn't see them. I took a few months off diving before going back to geoducks, but I still couldn't see those indents in the bottom. Then all of a sudden one day I could see them. By the end of that season I was making 2,500 bucks a week, an incredible wage for a twenty-year-old.

Scott Petersen and Jeff Sparks, both sea urchin divers on board the *Kuroshio*, get a first look at the intimidating dive site off Lacy Island.
David McRae photo

The diving industry is a lot of fun and very physical, but it is also quite dangerous, and about halfway through my first week diving, the captain on the dive boat next to us drowned. All the conditions were excellent for diving, so this was really frightening. I didn't dive for a week after that and I seriously evaluated whether I wanted to go back in the water. I knew that we lost one or two guys a year in the business, but to have a guy from the next boat drown was different.

Of course, when you're young like we were, you're always out partying all night. We'd leave Tofino in the morning, and it would take us about an hour-and-a-half to get out to the diving grounds—and all of us would be hungover. But the danger when you're hungover is forgetting things. One of the guys jumped overboard and, boom, he's back on the surface rolling around. He could hardly move. He was so hungover he'd forgotten to put the regulator in his mouth, and he'd gone all the way down to fifty feet and almost collapsed his lungs.

There's a crazy bunch in this industry—they're not called "bubbleheads" for nothing. Once—this was before my time—Ron Kelehare went out to dive with a tender on his boat, and when Mike Featherstone left in his boat a little later, he saw this little figure in the water waving away, and it was Ron Kelehare floating out to sea. Something had happened to his air supply and he'd had to bail out. His tender didn't see him because he was sitting on the deck smoking pot, having a little toke, a real no-no. So Mike picked Ron out of the water and then got on the radio and called up the tender and asked how his diver was doing. Ron was doing fine, the tender said, though

Divers on the swim grid of the *Kuroshio* pose for a photo at Virago Sound on the Queen Charlotte Islands. Many people think divers must be a bit crazy to do this job.
David McRae photo

he hadn't dropped off a bag in a while. So Mike pulled his boat up beside Ron's, and Ron jumped into his boat yelling at the tender, "How dare you?" The tender couldn't figure out what was going on.

I dove at one time for Larry Dougan, a very interesting fellow and a good hard worker. We were diving off Ucluelet and ran into a wolf eel. I got out of the water because I didn't want this thing to bite me, but Larry was really a hairy-assed fisherman, a true-blue old salt. So he went down after it and the wolf eel started hitting him in the chest. Something must have made this thing angry because it was really going at him and he never did get it. We could hear him yelling out of his regulator as he was coming out of the water.

Bliss Fawcett was another one of the guys I worked with. He dived with what was almost a hard hat, a thing called a Kirby Morgan. It's a huge helmet with straps that tie it in place around the neck. He was one of the first guys that ever dived for geoducks. An incredible man. He was diving just outside of Tofino at a place called Elbow Bank when this octopus came at him, just rolling across the sand with its tentacles coming out in front of it. He thought that it was so beautiful, but next thing he knew this bloomin' octopus was on top of him, on his head, and all over him. So he thought he'd just take it back to the boat and eat it. But when he tried to climb into the boat, the octopus grabbed onto the hull and then grabbed his helmet and started tearing it off. He could feel the tentacles going up under his mask and along the side of his face. He finally got it off and it got away. Scared the livin' daylights out of him.

We were always eating fish and having great barbecues. We'd grab abalone and scallops from the rocks. Often we would get Puget Sound box crabs. They're just massive, up to a foot-and-a-half across and about eight inches thick. The chunk of meat you can get out of one pincer weighs about a pound. We'd get them from time to time and boil them up. They were great. Dungeness crabs are pretty fast so you really have to go after them. I was diving one time up near Rivers Inlet, harvesting geoducks, and my arm was in the hole right up to my shoulder when hundreds of these crabs started coming out of the bottom right by my face. They bury themselves in the sand and fish like that. The only thing you see of the Dungeness crab is a line and two eyes sticking out of the sand.

Sometimes we'd get hold of a fish by the tail and bring it to the surface. There's one called a cabezon, like a cod, a stubby fish that can get pretty big—seventy to ninety pounds—but they're territorial as hell. When you're diving, all of a sudden these things will start attacking you. You'll see them coming out of the corner of your eye. They can't do any damage, but they're annoying, bouncing off your mask and such. Once, when Reuben Nunnez was diving with us, there was one hanging around, being really annoying, and he'd had enough of it. From the deck we could see him coming up the line, and it was taking him a long time. Then we realized that he had this fish by the tail. He'd used his dive knife and killed it. We ate it.

We used to have great annual Fisherman Balls up here in Tofino and in other places. Hundreds of people would come from all over BC. Everyone would go out and fish clams and oysters and geoducks and butter clams and abalone. All this stuff is illegal now unless you have a licence. You can't even possess them. Eventually the Fisherman Balls just stopped. It was too bad, because they were very community-oriented events.

Once, we were after geoducks just outside Prince Rupert at a place called Calamity Bay on the south end of Banks Island beside Terror Point. It was beautiful clear water and we were down anywhere from thirty to seventy feet, and there were big halibut everywhere. I've never ever seen anything like it. Sometimes our water pressure hit the geoducks the wrong way and they exploded. The guts would go all over the place and that's what these halibut were eating. We were there for three weeks. Near the last day of our stay, one big halibut got so bold that it grabbed the thumb of one of our divers and tried to rip it off, probably thinking it was a chunk of geoduck. It tore the glove right off of his hand. He came out of the water and said, "That's it! I'm not going through this any more!"

My brother and I were diving at MacIntosh Bay, just outside of Tofino, with him on one side of the rocks and me on the other. All of a sudden something hit him from behind. He turned around, thinking it was me, but there was nobody around. This thing hit him again and drove his face into the sand. He had no idea what it was. When he looked around there was a one-ton sea lion about four inches from his face. He wasted no time getting up to the boat. When I finished the day down there, he told me what had happened. I hadn't seen a thing. We had a great laugh over that.

We'd hear the orcas from time to time—they sounded like clothesline pulleys—but I never saw them. One day I came up and the tender asked if I'd seen the killer whales. They'd been circling and diving above me for about two hours. I've never heard of a whale attacking anybody.

Diver Tony Mulhall is on his way to check the quality of the sea urchins down below while diver Paul MacNeil stands by and awaits Tony's report.
David McRae photo

The first year I was diving we lived on the beach at a beautiful place called Turquot Island at Spider Anchorage. We used to work out of there for a month or so for several years. A couple of islands away from it there was a big wolf colony, and we could hear the wolves howling all night long.

I always dove from open skiffs. We'd work hard and at the end of the day we'd go back to the live-aboard. But one year, when Quinten Edwards was my tender, we didn't have a live-aboard. This was okay while I was diving out of Hakai Pass because we found a sports fishing camp, which was great, but when we went in around Ivory Island, about an hour above Bella Bella, and fished one of the inlets there, we lived on the beach. This was November and it was so cold that when we dived we would break the ice and go under it along the sides of the little bays. Every night we'd come in, anchor the boat out, and take turns to swim in to the beach and bring the boat in. We made a little plastic house, put some plywood down for a floor, and put a little space heater in there. We bought our supplies at a local hardware store. The only problem was that this was grizzly bear country. We had a fire going all night long, and we took turns getting up and tending it. We always expected to wake up with a griz in our faces.

I dived for geoducks for ten years and gradually drifted into sea urchins. I was good at it, and since it was pretty well just me at that time, I was able to pick the areas with high recovery rates. I could do anywhere from eight to ten thousand pounds a day and made money hand over fist. It was a good industry. Had a lot of fun.

Diving for sea cucumbers was an interesting industry, too. I had a boat called the *Sowhet*, and I walked every square inch of the islands in Clayoquot Sound, around every island. There were sea cucumbers everywhere. The first year I did a half-a-million pounds. Working off Port Hardy, there were two other divers with me, and I came in with over seventeen thousand pounds of sea cucumbers in one day. I couldn't believe it. My best day before that was about four-and-a-half thousand pounds. I ran into this tiny bay between two islands, about 40 feet wide and 150 feet long. It had a little channel about fifteen feet wide and two feet deep, and it was covered with sea cucumbers. The whole length of it. I sat there all day. I think I made about $12,000 in that one day.

Growing up to forty centimetres (sixteen inches) in length, sea cucumbers are harvested predominantly for the Chinese market.

Rick Harbo photo

Divers Paul McNeil (left) and Tony Mulhall (right) on the dive vessel *Kuroshio* exchange empty scuba tanks for full ones and enjoy a few moments of early morning calm in Sidney Inlet, Tofino, before returning to their underwater task.
David McRae photo

If people wanted to work for me, I would agree to train them but would not guarantee them a job at the end of their training. I had one guy show up, a very intelligent person with every kind of dive certificate you could think of, but within the first week he almost killed himself a couple of times. Finally I pulled him aside and told him that he could tend on the boat but would only get into the water if it was a beautiful, perfect day because I knew that he would have an accident. I didn't want to be responsible for it, and I didn't think that he was cut out for this industry. Oh, he was angry at me, but the reality was that he would have killed himself. He tried to work on some other boats and finally moved on and did something else. Safety has always been an issue for me. What price do you place on a person's life?

One year we had all been doing decompression dives, where you stay down past the allotted time and you have to hang and decompress. We were doing fifty-foot tables, so we had two 'decos' a day. At the end of our second dive, I was working on one side of the boat and the other diver on the other. I was just finishing off my decompression at the ten-foot level, and I watched him come up all the way from the bottom to the boat without stopping. I went up to the surface and told him, "You'd better get back in the water and hang." He got mad and said that he was fine, that he had only been working at forty feet. Five minutes later he had the spinal bends and was paralyzed from the waist down for a month. But he was very, very lucky. His problem was caused by the fact that he had put his depth gauge on the regulator hose that led to his mouth, and when he was reading the depth he would stand up. But he was six feet tall so when he read forty feet, it was really over forty-five feet, putting him into the fifty-foot range.

Another guy built what we called a suicide pack, jumped over the side of the boat and didn't have any air. It was turned off at the deck and he didn't have a bailout bottle of air on his backpack. Twenty minutes later the people on the boat noticed that there was nothing going on, so they pulled the guy up and he was dead. He had checked his air before he went down, taking in three or four breaths, but that air had been just sitting in the line. There was nothing left in it when he dived. We had a similar thing happen a couple of years later. A diver jumped away from the boat and accidentally dropped his weights, but they landed on his airline and pulled him to the bottom. He lived for about forty-five minutes after we hauled him up. A real tragedy. Just a simple little error.

When you're dealing with foreign environments, accidents are usually fatal or they cripple a person for life. In any emerging industry there's not enough money to go around and safety concerns don't always get attention. Today there's enough money in the industry for the owners to provide first-class boats, and all of the equipment is kept up. Divers make enough money so that they can afford to have dry suits rather than wetsuits. But I never trusted anyone else's equipment. My life was on the line, so when I'd get on a new boat, I'd tear the equipment apart and put it together again to my satisfaction.

Now there are a lot fewer deaths because the Workers Compensation Board in consultation with the industry has developed guidelines that really help in eliminating accidents. For example, now you go down following a down line. You don't jump away from the boat and freefall because then you have nothing to hold onto to climb back up. But we also butted heads with the WCB sometimes. They didn't always agree with the way we were working. We were harvesting sea cucumbers out of the Queen Charlottes when all of a sudden this Workers Compensation boat shows up out in the middle of nowhere. The guy said that he would have to shut

me down. I just told him to do his job and I'd do mine. I jumped back in the water and he was horrified. I believed that he was being overzealous.

In my seventeen years of diving there was never a death on any of my own boats, but on the boats that I ran we had one accident. The owner had outfitted this boat with an old compressor that didn't have proper air filters. As a result, it had passed oil from broken rings, and one of the divers, a man we called Clambo, got pneumonia because he breathed in the oil and it prevented air from getting to the air sacs in his lungs. It almost killed him. We were in the north island of the Queen Charlottes at the time, and he came up and said he wasn't feeling very well. His face was all red and white spots, and he was having a hard time getting his breath. He didn't get any better, and when he started convulsing, I realized what was happening and got on the phone. Right away the US Coast Guard Dive Fleet from Ketchikan, Alaska, got onto the American Coast Guard and said that they had a full dive team with a portable recompression chamber and could be there in twenty minutes, so I said come right away. Then the Canadian Coast Guard got involved and they caused havoc with the American Coast Guard because they told them that they had the situation under control and we would not be needing their service.

Surface-supply air lines, or "hookahs," can be up to seventy-five metres (two-hundred-fifty feet) long. They keep the diver connected to an oxygen tank on the boat and free him from carrying heavy oxygen tanks on his back.
Rick Harbo photo

The sea urchin fleet at Normansell Islands prepares for a windy night. The live-aboards are anchored in the middle and the aluminum dive skiffs are on the outside.

David McRae photo

But in reality they didn't have it under control, and we had to commandeer a plane from one of the big fishing lodges, the Oak Bay Marine Group, to fly the guy to Queen Charlotte City. The Coast Guard were supposed to have the Medevac jet meet him there but it was delayed for seven hours. So it took him about ten hours to get to Vancouver and a recompression chamber. He made it but was pretty sick for a while.

One time my boat was one of a group going from Bella Bella to the Queen Charlottes. I had the biggest boat—seventy tons, sixty-nine feet—and was towing one dive boat along behind it and had another one on deck. It usually takes eleven hours to cross Hecate Straits. It's an ugly place because there's no place to run except Vancouver Island or Alaska. At first the weather was nice, then it started blowing and got worse and worse and worse. We would fall over at the top of a wave, then ski down on the side of the hull for about 150 or 200 feet, the boat would come up, and we'd do that all over again on the next wave. We did this for about two hours and finally I decided that I'd had enough. We all turned around and got back to Aristazabel Island and anchored in Devlin Bay. By this time the smaller boats were low on gas so we decided to run up to Prince Rupert. An hour into that trip one of the guys snapped his drive shaft. It was lucky it happened there because if it had happened out on the strait we would have had to pull him off his boat and he would have lost it. Instead, we towed him all the way to Prince Rupert.

One trip up Grenville Channel the wind was blowing about seventy knots southeast, just shrieking, and the engine of one of the other boats seized up about an hour from a safe harbour. They wanted me to pull them off the boat but I said I'd tow them. I had a good long rope on board, I put a scotchman [bobber] on the end of it and floated it down to them, they attached it to their anchor winch, and we set off. We were big enough that the waves weren't really bothering us, but this guy was half our size. All of a sudden we heard them on the radio screaming that they were going under. A big wave had come over them and we were pulling them along like a submarine. When we finally got into Prince Rupert and were sitting in the bar, the guy from the boat, Al, came up to me and said, "This beer is for saving my life." Then with the next beer he said, "Now you're indebted to me for the rest of your life."

Working up north a lot of the guys would have what they called "safety meetings" in the bar. They'd party. But I figured that I was a thousand miles away from home so I was going to work. I would dive for two weeks or so and then go home for a week. Subsequently all the guys who worked with me made a lot of money. And many of these other guys would be broke. Once in a two-day period we pulled in fifty-two thousand pounds of product—just three divers, me and two other guys—and loaded it on the packer boat. They just loved us because usually we provided half their load.

The packers moved continuously between the port and us when we were too far away from land to deliver it ourselves. They were important to the fisheries, though not so much now because the fisheries have slowed down to the point that they can handle their own product. If you eliminate the packer, you're eliminating anywhere from fifteen to fifty cents a pound, depending on how far you have to travel. Salmon fishers still use packers because the fish have to be delivered daily.

In those days I was diving fall, winter and spring, and doing salmon in the summer with my little gillnetter. One of my business partners was a Seventh Day Adventist and they don't work from Friday night to Saturday night, their Sabbath. This was a real issue because I was not a religious type and I'd go out and fish while he'd sit on the boat. One winter we did some log salvaging up above Bella Bella out into Thomson Bay, towing the logs with our big boat and fishing with our smaller gillnetter, but when it came to the Sabbath, he wanted all of us to take the day off. I told him that I believed in choice: he could sit there and read his bible if he wanted to but I was going to work. This really bothered him. Finally I said, "Look, we need some fuel. Do you want to take the boat on the Sabbath and pick up fuel?" So he did that. To get from Thomson Bay to

Early in the day the *Kuroshio's* deck begins to fill with bags of sea urchins, each bag weighing about a hundred kilograms (two-hundred-twenty pounds).
David McRae photo

Shearwater and the gas station was a four-and-a-half-hour run, but there's a really tiny pass about twenty-five feet wide that you can get your boat through at high tide that cuts off almost three hours of running each way. So he went through there and spent the whole day at Shearwater. On the way back he got stuck on the rocks in the middle of this pass and called me on the phone to come and get him. So I got over there with the towboat and pulled him off. In the process we tore a hole in the stern of his boat. It took about three minutes for it to sink. I'm telling you, this guy will never work on the Sabbath again. God definitely sent him a message.

When I got tired of fishing and diving, I became a cash buyer and bought clandestinely for many of the big companies. They put the money in my pocket and I went and bought the fish for cash. But I really enjoyed the dive fishery. I stopped because I wasn't seeing my kids enough—I guess I saw them for two years out of ten altogether—and I really wanted to spend some time with them. But when I was diving I saw some wonderful underwater sights, like wolf eels and sharks. I have no regrets. I would like to dive again.

As a youth, Dave Sweeney began sport diving with his father near their home in Nanoose. For a number of years after he moved to Nanaimo he worked for a friend who owned the Sundown Diving store, though he eventually worked with two other diving companies as well. He qualified for his commercial diving certificate in 1985 and did commercial diving for about three years, harvesting red sea urchins all the way up the coast and in Georgia Strait. Later he managed the Duffin Cove Resort at Tofino for his former diving employer, Steve Dennis. He left in 2006.

Initially I worked with one diveboat owner but left after one season because of some unfortunate experiences with him. On my first trip with him to harvest sea cucumbers, while we were still at the wharf in Port Hardy, the skippers of several other commercial boats tied up there were all saying not to leave as there was a bad storm coming. However, the boss insisted that we had to make it to the dive site up near Bella Bella and we were going to go, no matter what. We were in one heck of a wild storm across Queen Charlotte Sound. My aluminum diving-boat, which was towed behind his packer, didn't even run, and we broke loose twice, actually tearing in half the two fourteen-inch steel-belted tires that were our shock absorbers where the line was attached to the next boat. The two guys with me were extremely seasick, couldn't even move, so I was the only one that could get out and try to tie us back up again. I decided that if I was going to go outside the cabin in the middle of the night on Queen Charlotte Sound in that hell of a storm, I was going to go out wearing my dry suit. I figured that if I went in the water, I might live to talk about it because I would be able to maintain my body heat. So I went out to the front of the diveboat and the big packer backed up to it, and I actually had to throw one of the steel-belted tires up onto the top deck of the boat with it pitching in the storm and its great big prop about fifteen feet in front of my face. I was hoping that they weren't going to back right over us. We did manage to get the tire up onto the top deck on the third try and all of the poly rope with it. We got tied up and took off but after about an hour we broke loose again. We got ourselves tied up for the second time and finally got into some calm water. We kind of licked our wounds, and I decided that it wasn't something that I ever wanted to do again. I quickly realized how little respect the owner/operator of these boats had for Mother Nature. It was the kind of experience that you never forget.

We worked in that area for two or three days, with all of the cucumbers being loaded onto the packer. When it reached a full load, the boss said that we had to get to the next opening, which was in the Queen Charlottes. So we had to travel across Hecate Strait, which is an absolutely horrible stretch of water. We left from Aristazabel

Dave Sweeney has fond memories of his diving years.
Donna Sweeney photo

Lacy Island is located off the west coast of
Langara Island, at the northern tip of the Queen
Charlotte Islands. When a huge groundswell is
hammering the shore like this, sea urchin
harvesting is impossible.
David McRae photo

Island but after an hour, realizing that we weren't going to make it
across, we turned around and it took us six-and-a-half hours to get
back to the spot we left from. Once again the boss had tied the boats
together, obviously trying to save fuel, and on the way back I watched
the packer boat turn over on its side. I felt that if I had been near
enough, I could have pushed it right over and turned it upside down.
If the load had shifted in the hold, that boat would have gone down,
and we were tied to it and I wouldn't have had a chance to get off
our boat or even to get into my dry suit. Anyhow, we waited for
better weather and finally got across. After we got back from working
in the Charlottes, I realized that I no longer wanted to work for this
man. The next opportunity I had to get on a packer boat, I decided
I was going home. So I packed up all my gear, jumped on the boat
and radioed out to my former boss. I told him that I wasn't working
for him anymore, that he was too much of a threat to my life and that
there was no money in the world worth risking my life for. His
language was unrepeatable.

I worked at a dive shop in Nanaimo for about a year, then got
hooked up with a gentleman by the name of Steve Dennis and
started diving for him. He was a totally different person from my first
boss, wonderful to work for, and he treated us really well. On the
previous job nine of the twelve guys were straight out of jail, where
the guys on Steve's crew were all very hard-working. He had a few

very simple rules: no guns, no drugs, no alcohol on his boat at any time, no matter if you were an invited guest or not. We wore quarter-inch neoprene suits with clothes underneath. We spent our time running on the bottom, which is why we didn't wear fins and why we wore so much lead weight on our backs to keep us from rising. We got up at the crack of dawn, were working before the sun came up, and we didn't get out of the water until it was starting to get dusk. We made a tremendous amount of money and worked extremely hard for it. Steve is a really good guy. He taught us a lot about the ocean, about reading charts, and made us feel very comfortable. If he had fallen off the boat, any one of us could have brought it home. He had a great respect for nature and never, ever, took any chances with anyone's life. I worked for him for almost three years and kept in very close contact afterwards.

Most urchin diving is done in fairly shallow water—you tend to be in the surf line up to thirty feet down—so the tender and I would jump into the skiff just as the sun was coming up and we'd run along the shorelines with the ladder over the side, surveying for good urchin beds. I was in my suit hanging onto the ladder, face down in the water. If we found kelp patches, we would generally find lots of urchins because kelp is their food. Wherever we found them, we had to go down to see if they were good because if they don't have an adequate kelp food source they don't produce roe. Then they have just muddy water inside instead of that nice banana-yellow roe.

The skiff carries a compressor with a tank for air that is fed down to the divers. We had a boom and a small davit on the side of the boat, which allowed us to attach a rope to the boat. We would send two small bags down to the bottom on a quarter-inch poly line. Each of these bags had a big metal ring around the top and a big pink scotchman with no air in it. Part of our backpack system allowed us to have one line where we could shoot some air into this bobber. We'd go around the bottom with the bag in one hand, keeping it on its side, and a custom-made metal rake in the other. It was made to the right width so that we knew we were picking urchin of the correct size limit. We would go around knocking urchins off the rocks and stuffing the bag until they started falling out. Then we'd take our air hose and give our little scotchman a shot of air. It would fill up a bit and become neutrally buoyant so that it would hold the bag upright on the bottom. When the bag was almost full, we'd knock one urchin off the rocks, stick it to one hand, then bang fifteen or twenty more of them off and stick them all together to top the bag up. When it was full enough, we'd give the scotchman a last blast of air and it would head for the surface. Meanwhile, we'd start filling the second bag and by the time it was full the tender would be sending the empty bag down. He'd pull the full bags out of the water with the boom and empty them onto the skiff's floor. Then he'd shovel the urchins into large bags—about eight feet tall—that would hold about a thousand of them. We had a big A-frame attached to the boat's gunnels to hold these big bags up. Once the skiff was full, that was it for the day, and we transferred them to the big packer boat.

Our average bottom time per day was seven to eight hours; the only time we went to the surface was to use the washroom or have a bite to eat. From time to time we'd actually pick the anchor up underwater and drag the boat to where we were working, plunk the anchor down and carry on. It was piecework so the more urchins we picked, the more money we made. But when you're a long way from your home and family—our trips were four weeks out and two weeks home—you might as well be making lots of money. A good diver on the coast could average six to eight thousand pounds worth of product in a day, and we got paid thirty cents a pound. I figure I averaged $800 to $1,000 a day. Once when we were working around Tofino, Steve and I went out for the day and I came in with about 8,500 pounds worth of product, an extremely good day for me. Steve was the last diver to come in and had picked about 17,800 pounds that day. He was very efficient underwater.

I dived for sea cucumbers around Aristazabel Island, Bella Bella and around the Charlottes. We picked them in the same way as the urchins. There's really not a lot in the cucumbers. They're full of seawater inside with fine strips of meat. They're very tasty, but my first experience with them was like chewing on an army boot. I guess I didn't prepare it very well.

I had some neat experiences underwater. On one trip in the Charlottes I was chased off the spot where I was diving by a sculpin that was no more than three or four inches long. This little fellow was determined to chase me off. Every time I turned around he was biting at my lips or nose and banging on my mask. I guess I was in his territory. After about a half-hour of this I gave up. I couldn't put up with anymore of his BS.

I saw some incredible scenery, including seals and sea lions. I did have a phobia about killer whales but never did see any. I dived very closely with grey whales and a calf. We saw lots of things on the bottom, everything from cabezons to octopus. I got quite a few Alaska king crabs in the Charlottes—I ate one every couple of days. Once when I was sport-diving with my dad off Nanoose we saw several Steller sea lions. The females are very flirtatious, try to get close to you, bite your fins and do anything they can to get your attention, but the bulls tend to take offence to that. They're very protective of their harems and will charge you. They're clumsy on land but can really fly underwater, and they weigh from fifteen hundred to two thousand pounds, so they're quite scary when they come at you. They turn away about an inch from your head.

Swimming scallops are interesting. I encountered some when I went sport diving outside of Nanaimo. I came down the anchor line and disturbed the bottom. They must have considered themselves in some kind of a threat, so a whole school of them started swimming. They're the funniest looking things—like a set of dentures swimming around backwards, opening and closing their shells. There's not a lot of meat in them, something smaller than a dime inside. They're quite tasty, but I think the rock scallops are better. They're fixed to the rocks and have a lot more meat in them.

I had one unforgettable experience while we were diving off Aristazabel Island, off Bella Bella. We'd done quite a bit of surveying for urchins that day, most of it unsuccessful, and I was a little frustrated because we didn't have any product. Finally, with the day half over, we found a spot where there were lots of urchins and kelp, and I decided to go down. I put my backpack on—it contains a small pony bottle for extra air—my regulator, and somewhere between 90 and 110 pounds of weight. And then it happened. I stumbled going over the side of the boat and went head first—instead of feet first—over the side with a hundred pounds of lead on my back and dived straight to the bottom. The backpack slid up my back, and all the air that was in my suit went to my feet and legs. I couldn't turn myself over. I was lying head first on the bottom underneath the skiff, trying to decide what to do to get myself straightened around. I could still breathe, had the regulator in my mouth, was still getting air from the surface, but when you're upside down in a dry suit, there's no air around your chest. A dry suit only has vents to release the air on either your arm or your chest, depending where you put the valve. This is so you can vent your suit for comfort but also to equalize the air and water pressure so you're neutrally buoyant. That allows you to walk on the bottom naturally. If you stay upside down too long, your feet end up where your knees should be in the suit. You just bulge to the point where you look like the Big-O Tire Man.

I tried everything I could, including bending my knees to my chest and trying to roll myself over to get air back into the chest of my suit so I would rise, until I was pretty well exhausted. But I still couldn't right myself, and, of course, there was three hundred feet of line attached to me, including the air hose and the half-inch poly line, so I couldn't possibly pull all that line out of the skiff when I was right underneath it. The tender didn't know what was going on. He could see the bubbles, knew I was right underneath the boat, and thought I was down there picking urchins. Next thing you know, my mask started getting a little bit of water in it. I thought, okay, when you're standing on the bottom upright, and you get a bit of water in your mask, you tilt the bottom of it. So I thought, seeing I'm upside down, the reverse should be the solution to the problem, so I lifted the top part of my mask to try and blow all the water out, but instead it flooded. Now I couldn't see much of anything, although I could still see the hull of the boat overhead drifting in the current. Now what could I do?

I put a bit more air in my suit, thinking that maybe I could float feet-first back up to the surface, but that didn't work. So I unclipped myself out of my backpack and held it with one hand. I was in only about twenty-five or thirty feet of water, and it would be easy enough to do an emergency ascent, but I was afraid that I was going

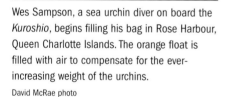

Wes Sampson, a sea urchin diver on board the *Kuroshio*, begins filling his bag in Rose Harbour, Queen Charlotte Islands. The orange float is filled with air to compensate for the ever-increasing weight of the urchins.

David McRae photo

to hit the bottom of the boat. I figured at that point that I'd exhausted every strategy I could think of to get out of this mess, so I might just as well just drop the backpack. As soon as I let go, with my suit absolutely full of air, I rocketed up, hit the bottom of the boat and stuck there like a starfish. Then I had to clamber out from underneath still holding my breath and get to surface. The tender had no idea what had hit the boat—the compressor was still running and all the gauges were showing properly. I climbed out from underneath, got my first breath of air, and at that point was so exhausted I'd had enough for the day.

On one trip we were moving our live-aboard—the *Christian Joy*, a fifty-two-foot seine boat—from Coal Harbour on Vancouver Island to Port Hardy, which meant we had to go around Cape Scott. We dragged one of the skiffs—a thirty-two-footer—and a second one was lashed up on top of the seine drum. The weather report from Vancouver said that the weather was mild with low seas and low wind, but we were about an hour and a half into the trip when the weather got incredibly bad with winds and high seas. The skiff we were towing spent most of its time in the air because, no matter how we lengthened or shortened the tow line, the timing was never quite right. It took us about five hours of solid green water to get to Cape Scott. We notified Vancouver about their incorrect report.

We were just about around Cape Scott when the diesel stove plugged up and filled most of the cabin's inside with black smoke. We shut that down. Then a twelve-foot herring punt that had been under the seine drum broke loose on the deck. We idled the motor, pointed the boat into the wind and Jeff and I ran back to tie the skiff down. One of the tenders who was with us couldn't move—he was so green, so seasick. We got back into the wheelhouse and powered up, but when we looked back, we could see the two lines towing the skiff behind us were straight down into the water. We figured that we had lost the skiff for sure, but the skipper told me that he had towed sunken skiffs before, and that this was not the place to deal with it. We carried on, heading for shallow water where we might be able to pull it back up. We'd dragged it underwater for about an hour before we got into the inner channel heading toward Hardy when all of a sudden we felt something just let go. We dragged up the two towlines and recovered two big aluminum plates and the stainless steel bridle system that had been welded to the front of the boat. Someone found the rest of that skiff about a year later. I didn't enjoy that trip but it was all part of living and working on the ocean.

Into the Bottom of the Sea

Sedco 135F Oil Drilling Rig

"One time we were trying to lift the anchor over the stern and the nylon line stretched to such a point that it was like a length of hard steel. It suddenly snapped and, like a rubber band with the speed of a bullet, whipped the wheelhouse, smashing and badly damaging the lifeboat that was secured thwartships aft of the wheelhouse. It just missed the other skipper where he was standing at the outside controls and went between the two crew members who were standing on the other side of him. Had it hit one of us, we would have been split down the middle."

Captain Harold Monks

The *Sedco 135F* drilling rig was located offshore from Vancouver Island in the summer of 1967. The helipad, pipe racks, mud and storage tanks, and crew quarters are clearly visible. The drill floor, which is open to the elements, is surrounded by ancillary equipment and the offices of the drilling personnel.

Courtesy Shell Canada Limited Photographic Archives

The largest vessel of its kind in the world and the first to be constructed in Canada, the *Sedco 135F* offshore drilling rig was built between 1965 and 1967 at the Victoria Machinery Depot in BC at a cost of $10 million. The owner, Southeastern Commonwealth Drilling Ltd., leased it to Shell Canada for exploratory gas and oil drilling along the west coast of Vancouver Island, north into Queen Charlotte Sound and in Hecate Strait. Drilling was carried out on this semi-submersible or "jack up" rig while it floated on three huge pontoons that were about eighty feet below the water's surface at the base of its supporting legs or caissons.

Tommy Mitchell, who worked on the *Sedco 135F* while it was in BC waters, recalled that "the drilling platform was huge for that time, built in the shape of a triangle with three large columns, one on each corner of the triangle, supporting the platform. Each column,

During the construction of the rig, large Murphy Pacific cranes were used to lift sections into place during assembly.

Courtesy Shell Canada Limited Photographic Archives

approximately thirty feet in diameter, was in turn supported by a large pontoon. The level of the structure and the depth at which it sat in the water was controlled by ballasting and deballasting the pontoons. For stability, the drilling platform sat low in the water during drilling operations, minimizing the effects of the wave and swell actions. When moving from one drilling site to another, the rig was raised to sit high in the water for easy towing. The drilling equipment on the *Sedco 135F* was of the standard variety, similar to that used on a land-based operation. Its machinery was powered by electric motors, the power being supplied by generators run by diesel motors, hence the name 'diesel-electric rig'."

Once it was ballasted, the rig sat low in the water in its drilling position.
Courtesy Shell Canada Limited Photographic Archives

Trained as a geological engineer, Lee Slind joined Shell Oil in 1954 and became part of an exploration team that undertook the daunting task of mapping the geology of the entire west coast of Vancouver Island.

Courtesy Lee Slind

By early 1967 the rig was almost completed, and the cars of eager employees lined the dock.

Courtesy Shell Canada Limited Photographic Archives

Lee Slind, after completing a degree in geological engineering, joined Shell Canada in Calgary in 1954. He had exploration assignments in all of the frontier areas of Canada and worked with Shell International in the North Sea and the Middle East. Retiring from Shell in 1984, he joined a small exploration consulting company and continued his adventurous life working in Nepal, the Philippines, East Africa and again on the Canadian frontiers. He lives with his wife, Joann, in Cochrane, Alberta.

I was a senior geologist working for Shell Canada as a member of a seismic operations group that consisted of a district geologist, who was our boss, three to six geologists, a seismic party chief, three to six geophysicists and from four to eight technical staff. We were the main folks in the field and did most of the company's work at sea.

Oil seeps and oil shales had been noted along the West Coast since the early 1900s, and oil and gas exploration had been conducted there since at least 1914. Before we came along, the Geological Survey of Canada and the BC Department of Energy and Mines had been mapping the onshore for a number of years and realized the oil and gas potential. Competitor companies had explored the adjacent onshore areas and drilled on the Queen Charlotte and Gulf Islands and in the Fraser Delta, but unfortunately there were no discoveries.

In the late 1950s and early 1960s the oil discoveries in Alaska near Anchorage, the developments off California and the oil and gas shows along the Washington and Oregon coast and the Gulf of Alaska encouraged the Shell Oil Company to expand their exploration to the north. Canada has a significant continental shelf and large coastal basins that could contain enormous volumes of attractive sediments. Furthermore, at this time exploration and development obligations in the US were quite onerous, only allowing five-year licensing periods, which is much too short a time for orderly exploration. In Canada the rules gave the companies a longer time to explore offshore, so in 1961 Shell Canada and a sister company, Shell Oil Company, filed for drilling rights on approximately twelve million offshore acres of Canada Lands, and the West Coast exploration program began.

The following year the emphasis was on arranging for support services. This included contracting for tug and supply boats, establishing supply depots, planning access to onshore survey stations, contacting positioning (survey) contractors and having aeromagnetic and detailed aerial photography surveys flown. At the same time an innovative field geology program was conducted along the west coast of Vancouver Island. An older and well-used small coastal freighter was modified to hold a helicopter landing pad aft, and this ship served as the field party's base camp. The party consisted of four geologists (including myself), the helicopter pilot, a mechanic, the ship's cook, a seaman/helper and the ship's captain.

There were 9,000 tons of steel used in the construction of the *Sedco 135F*. Each side of the triangular main deck was 280 feet long; the deck rested on three caissons, each 35 feet in diameter. The structure was fastened to the seabed by nine anchors, each weighing 15 tonnes. Each link of the anchor chains weighed 120 pounds, for a total weight of 800 tonnes. The drilling equipment included a 142-foot mast with a 1,000,000-pound hook load capacity.

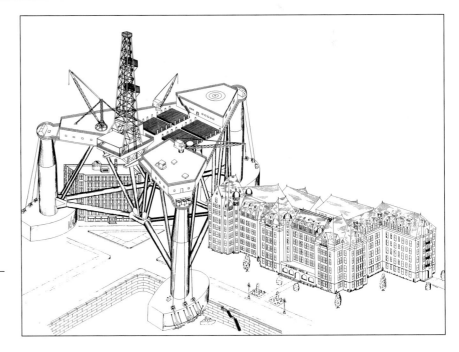

This diagram compares the size of the *Sedco 135F* to that of the Empress Hotel in Victoria, BC.

Courtesy Shell Canada Limited Photographic Archives

The *Min Tide* was one of the oil rig supply ships that tended the *Sedco 135F*.

Courtesy Captain Harold Monks

We moved the vessel south to north along the coast, anchoring frequently so that the geologists could be transported to examine the rocks along the shoreline. The woods were too thick and the underbrush too dense to allow for any meaningful trips further inland. We geologists would fan out along the beach areas, examining rock outcrops, collecting fossils and rock samples and making geological maps, then return to the freighter each night for meals and a rest.

This mapping exercise covered the entire west side of Vancouver Island, a formidable task, but the program's purpose was to determine what kind of sedimentary and igneous rock formed the coastal edge of the large sedimentary basin that lay to the west. It was hoped that the basin would contain the amount and kind of sediments that would be attractive for hydrocarbons, that is, oil and gas. A later seismic program could tell how thick the basin was and how the rocks were folded and faulted, but it could not tell us their make-up. A thorough combination of geological and geophysical techniques were, and are, essential in exploring any area. This mapping program was very successful, but we geologists were the butt of cruel jests from our co-workers stuck in Edmonton, who were jealous of those enjoying the West Coast, even though our crew worked twelve-hour days, seven days a week.

During 1963 an onshore velocity program was initiated on Vancouver Island to determine the rates at which sound is transmitted through various rock types and formations, and field mapping was carried out in the Gulf Islands. Shell also acquired additional acreage that year and we conducted seismic and bottom-sampling programs. This operation was strictly marine. Radio high-fix stations were located onshore to support the survey system, but all the rest was at sea. Our fleet consisted of a converted US warship, the *Miss Juanita,* the aging, wooden-hulled Canadian minesweeper *Cedarwood,* a shooting boat used to carry the crew involved in placing explosives

Life was not all heavy work. Here, two workers take time out for a bit of fun.
Courtesy Tommy Mitchell

in the water, and at times a Fisheries observation boat. There were a few "secondees" from Shell Oil US on board, but most of the seismic operators, surveyors and support were Canadian, farm boys to a large extent who had never been to sea, so there were a lot of "sick puppies" on these boats. One surveyor kept a wastebasket between his feet as he stared steadily at the survey monitor in front of him. No time to run for the rail; just use the wastebasket. I don't think that poor fellow has gotten over it yet.

Sick or not, they all did a fine job, and except for a few rare times when the boat had to run for a cove during a big blow, they worked through most everything. The *Miss Juanita* was fast and sleek but rolled rather badly I am told, but the vessel I was on, the *Cedarwood*, was slow and seemed to wallow. It carried the seismic system made up of an underwater electrical "sparker" and "gas exploder" that consisted of a series of twenty-foot-long hollow neoprene tubes that were repeatedly filled with an acetylene mixture. The gas was exploded within the tubes and the exhaust discharged. This happened every few seconds around the clock and provided a very good seismic source without harming any sea life. The noise was a little hard on sleep, but you could be in the instrument room and watch the seabed and its geology unfold beneath you. Instant gratification.

The *Cedarwood* also had the equipment to take sea-bottom sediment samples. The sampling device included nine thousand feet of one-and-a-half-inch steel cable attached to a six- to eight-hundred-pound weight welded to a four-foot length of steel pipe. The weight was lowered over the side and the cable run out. Once the pipe hit the bottom and dug in, it was pulled loose, hauled up and the sediment removed. The sample was treated to separate the living from old material and then sent to the lab. All in all, not a bad system and we retrieved several thousand samples.

One of our more exciting times was when we were sampling along the edge of the continental shelf in several thousand feet of water, and a Canadian military aircraft buzzed us. Things were confused, but it turned out that we were dropping this weighted pipe into a Canadian Navy ammunition dump. Nothing exploded, however.

We also exploded small dynamite charges in tidal pools to identify the rock types offshore. We measured the time it took for the sound of the explosion to travel through the different rock types. This went very well until we tried to get good exposure of the Triassic-age Metchosin volcanics, because it happened that their best exposure was in the vicinity of the William Head prison facility. We were finally able to get permission to conduct our experiments within the prison grounds, and the official permission on government letterhead stated, "You have permission to conduct the study, but please do not provide the prisoners with any explosives."

For some of our geologists the year 1963 was an especially good one because the field-mapping program moved from the west side of Vancouver Island to the Gulf Islands. The crew of four slept and ate at the Yellow Point Lodge, a very fancy tourist site at that time, and went to work each day in a high-powered speedboat. Their objective was to map the geology of the Gulf Islands, but their sub-objective, we jealous folks thought, was to see how long each of them could stay on their water skis while they went to their base.

The major work of 1964 was the large offshore seismic program carried out by two seismic parties. At the same time, sea bottom sampling and onshore seismic velocity studies continued. We also prepared a recommendation to drill eight wells in two years, using a semi-submersible rig; the estimated cost was $10.4 million.

Seismic and bottom-sampling programs were the main focus in 1966, the seismic being improved by better, stacked techniques. Recommendations for the first two drilling locations were presented, and these received approval a year later. Canada's first offshore well was now commissioned to drill, and the tug *Gulf Joan* towed the *Sedco 135F* with great ceremony from Victoria through the Strait of Juan de Fuca to a location offshore of Bamfield Inlet.

The drillers and engineers had some familiarity with the rig, but we geologists had to wait until it was on site. We didn't know what we were going to run into from a geological point of view. There were two geologists on board, me included, a micro-paleontologist for micro fossils, and a paleobotanist for pollen identification. The sample examination area was just great and the accommodations reasonable, but my, it was a long way down to the water. We got along well with the crews, and I was even permitted to climb the derrick to get a good look at the world.

All the wells in this part of the Olympic Basin were to be named after Greek gods and goddesses. Prometheus was the first named because he was the "fire bringer"—presumably gas- and oil-fired. The first well, Shell-Anglo Prometheus H-68, was spudded [began the drilling process] in June, and the work began. It was the usual practice to examine the drill samples at ten-foot intervals. In slow drilling country this is just fine as it takes a long time to drill ten feet of hard rock. The West Coast is very different. The section we drilled into was very soft and the drill bit virtually washed through it. Fantastic penetrations were achieved, so instead of one geologist or engineer looking at a sample every ten feet, we had an assembly line with four persons lined up, each one taking a sample from every forty feet. We believe a record was set—2,700 feet in twenty-four hours. Unfortunately, after such great progress the bit and pipe got stuck. Eventually drilling resumed but with caution.

The weather was highly variable out there, sometimes clear and calm but at other times quite the opposite. When the entire program was being developed, weather forecasting and the level of storm severity were carefully considered. The Canadian government had

The tug *Gulf Joan* is seen here towing the *Sedco 135F* to a new drilling position.

Courtesy Seaspan International Ltd.

onshore weather stations on Vancouver Island and elsewhere and a weather ship far out in the North Pacific Ocean, and based mainly on these sources a forecasting of expected weather was developed. Weather and sea conditions are measured in several ways, but the one that was often quoted was the concept of the "hundred-year storm," that is, a storm of such ferocity that supposedly it will only happen once in one hundred years. Well, although the *Sedco 135F* was designed to handle them, they are not pleasant to be in, and that vessel went through several hundred-year storms within the first year. We figured that we were at least four hundred years ahead of ourselves. After deliberation, it was concluded that forecasts based on a ship thousands of miles at sea and stations on shore had little accuracy to predict the weather in the shelf areas where the drilling was conducted. Lucky that nobody was lost. Safety was number one on the rig.

David Jones, Environment Canada: "On October 22, 1968, *Sedco 135F* was anchored just west of Cape St. James. Sixty-five-foot waves were battering the rig when a monster wave exposed a lower support form. The ensuing wave crest passed just below a control room positioned one hundred feet above the support form."

Construction of the *Sedco 135F* rig is seen under way in 1966 at the Victoria Machinery Depot. Due to the immense size of the rig, large pieces were constructed separately and then welded and bolted together.

Courtesy Shell Canada Limited Photographic Archives

Tommy Mitchell (left) worked on an Alberta drilling rig in his younger days. The working machinery is the same as that used on the *Sedco 135F* drill rig.

Courtesy Tommy Mitchell

In 1939 Tommy Mitchell left the Alberta farm where he had grown up to go to work in the Turner Valley oil patch. He worked his way up from roughneck on drilling rigs to the position of drilling foreman. But it was quite a change of scenery when he was assigned to the group drilling off the west coast of Vancouver Island from the Sedco drilling rig. He set up his home base in Victoria where the Shell operating office was located and then, to gain experience in offshore drilling, he worked as a trainee drilling foreman on a rig operating at various locations off the US west coast, commuting weekly from Victoria. Tommy has very detailed recall of his experiences on the Sedco 135F. He now lives with his wife, June, in Vernon, BC.

Most of the people working on the rig resided in Victoria. Transportation was normally by fixed-wing aircraft to Tofino and by helicopter from there to the rig. If conditions were such that the helicopter could not fly, the crews were taken by one of the rig supply vessels, the *Min Tide* or the *Canadian Tide*. The boat would tie up to the rig and the crew would be lifted up to the platform by crane using a device called a basket, which was made up of a padded ring about ten feet in diameter suspended by a lifting ring attached to the crane by a smaller ring. A series of six ropes approximately twelve feet long were fastened at one end to the small ring at the top and at the other end to the large ring at the bottom, thus forming the basket. The crane would lower it until the large ring was just touching the supply boat's deck. The men would stand on the large ring and hold onto the ropes that were attached to both rings and the whole thing would be lifted off the boat and set down on the rig floor where the

The *Sedco 135F's* crane and one of its supply boats are visible on the right-hand side of this photograph.
Courtesy Tommy Mitchell

men would just step off. This was usually a pretty harrowing operation as the boat would be moving around in the water from side to side and up and down with the wave action. This is where the crane operator's expertise came into play, as he had to pick the basket up at exactly the right moment off the boat's deck after the men had stepped onto the basket ring. Of course, the procedure would be reversed for the crew leaving the rig for their time off.

There were generally thirty-two to thirty-five people on board, and a few more during special operations. The total capacity of the rig was in the neighbourhood of forty people. All the crews worked twelve-hour shifts with some exceptions. Personnel included the five-man drilling crew—the driller, derrick man, Cat head man, tong man and back-up man. The driller operated the draw-works or hoist and was the hands-on man in charge of the actual drilling operation. He was also the boss of his crew while on shift. The derrick man was in charge of the mud and during the "round trip" of pulling all of the drill pipe out of the hole and running it back in after changing the twelve-and-a-quarter-inch bit. He worked in the derrick approximately eighty-five feet above the drill floor, racking ninety-foot sections of pipe as they were pulled out of the hole, disconnected and set back. The Cat head man was charged with looking after the motors and had his own special job when "round-tripping" the pipe. The floor men—tong and back-up tong—handled the tongs, which were the huge wrenches used to undo the pipe joints, spin the pipe out and rack it on the pipe-rack on the rig's floor. The tool pusher, or rig foreman, was the overall supervisor of the drilling crew. He was on twenty-four-hour call. When things were running smoothly he had a relatively easy job, but when there were problems with the rig he was expected to be on the job until everything was fixed or the problem solved, whether it took twenty-four, thirty-six or even forty-eight hours.

Some of our drilling problems related to the weather. At times the terrific storms we experienced made it impossible to continue drilling because of the rig's movement up and down as well as sideways and back and forth. At these times we would disconnect the pipe running from the ocean floor to the rig. The cables that supported the rig ran through pulleys that were solidly attached to the heavy weights that we called counter-balances.

The other personnel on the platform included a roustabout crew of five members, one of whom was the roustabout foreman. Their duties were pretty general in nature—keeping the entire platform

With the rig in position off the west coast of Vancouver Island, roughnecks "trip" the drill pipe on the floor of the *Sedco 135F* and slip the block into the top of the rotary table. Once the drill string is secured in this way, the upper part can be screwed on or off. To the right is a pair of tongs, a large wrench-like device that is used to either break or tighten the connections in the drill string. Courtesy Shell Canada Limited Photographic Archives

Tommy Mitchell (left) is deep in discussion
about operations at a drilling rig in Alberta in
1960.

Courtesy Tommy Mitchell

clean and tidy, loading and unloading supplies and stacking them in
their proper places. One aspect of their cleaning job was to deal with
the platform's dirty sides. The men sat in a special chair suspended on
the end of the crane line and were lowered over the side with a hose
and scrub brush in hand to wash the structure. Of course, there was
nothing between them and the wild, churning ocean below, but
while it appeared to be a very dangerous operation, it was not as bad
as it looked. Safety was always a prime concern during all operations

and there were very few injuries. And we did have a first aid man on board.

The kitchen and dining room operated twenty-four hours a day, so there were two cooks and two cooks' helpers working twelve-hour shifts. And a camp crew acted as male chambermaids, making the beds, cleaning the sleeping quarters and generally keeping the camp spic and span. The Shell people on board consisted of two drilling foremen, a geologist, a petroleum engineer and a drilling engineer. The Shell foreman's job was more overseer or watchdog, not directly supervisory, but he was there to make sure everything was carried out in an effective and efficient manner, conferring with and advising the rig tool pusher in many of the operations. Our job was to ensure that Shell's interests were first and foremost at all times.

To begin operations after the rig was positioned and anchored, we drilled approximately one thousand feet below the ocean floor,

The *Sedco 135F* could drill up to 12,000 feet (3657 metres) under the ocean floor. The drill pipe rotated from the surface and began with a nine-inch drill bit that was reduced in size until final depth was reached.

From a drawing by Tommy Mitchell

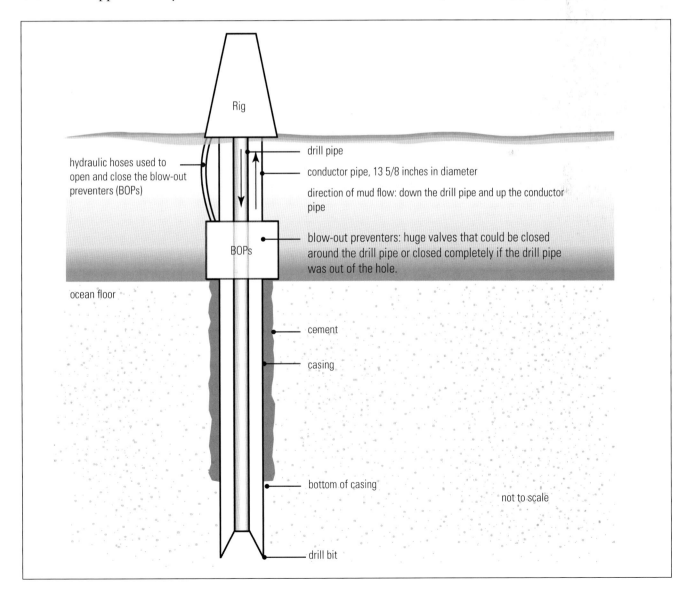

then ran and cemented in place one thousand feet of surface casing pipe, thirteen-and-five-eighths inches in diameter. The cement consisted of pure powdered dry cement mixed with water into a pumpable slurry. It was pumped down the inside of the casing, around the bottom of it and up the outside to the ocean floor. A check valve prevented the cement from flowing back into the casing while it set and hardened, thus providing a solid foundation for the blow-out preventers (BOPs). Attached to the casing was a set of four guidelines, which were heavy cables running from the ocean floor to the rig, each cable running through a pulley and attached to a heavy counterweight which kept the cables very taut. The BOPs were a set of huge valves that could be closed around the drill pipe or closed completely if the drill pipe was out of the hole. One function of the guidelines was to guide the BOPs to the ocean floor as they were lowered from the rig and latched to the surface casing by way of a special latching device. The function of the BOPs was to control any excess pressure encountered during drilling that could not be controlled by the weight of the drilling mud.

The drilling fluid, or mud as it is commonly called, had several functions. The primary one was to bring the drill cuttings to the surface as the mud was circulated down the inside of the five-inch drill pipe and up the outside or annulus, a space that was thirteen-and-three-eighths inches in diameter. The mud was then run through a screen, the cuttings were discarded and the mud was recirculated. Small samples of the cuttings were caught every ten feet and washed clean so the geologists could examine them through a microscope. Another of the mud's functions was to control any excess pressure in the shale, sandstone or limestone formation being drilled through that could cause a blowout. It also deposited a thin coat of plaster on the walls of the drill hole, helping to stabilize the formation and prevent sloughing into the hole.

The mud's properties ranged from pure water through various stages of thin slurry to a very thick, barely pumpable muck, depending on the drilling conditions at any one time. The thickness or viscosity of the mud was controlled by adding a very finely ground clay known as bentonite. If it was necessary to reduce the mud's viscosity, it could be done by adding water or special chemicals. The mud's weight or specific gravity was controlled by adding a finely ground material known as barite, which was much heavier than bentonite. The mud's condition and properties were critical at all times so its condition was monitored and adjusted by personnel who were highly trained in their trade and were known as mud men or mud engineers.

Captain Harold Monks, a former BC Coast Pilot, also worked for a time on one of the support vessels for the Sedco 135F.

In 1966 I was captain of the *Min Tide*, a twin-screw oil rig supply vessel 168 feet in length. Our job was to service and tow the *Sedco 135F* when it was test-drilling at various locations off the west coast of Vancouver Island and in Hecate Strait. Supply vessels were a combination of many things—tug, tanker, cargo ship and passenger ship—and the two identical vessels—the *Min Tide* and the *Canadian Tide*—were the project's workhorses. Regulations required one vessel to remain on standby duty close to the rig at all times in case of emergency, though this was usually the job of the tug *Gulf Joan*. In order to lie at the rig to deliver cargo, we would first run out an anchor with close to twenty shackles—1,800 feet of chain. This was twice the amount of chain that a normal ship was required to carry. Two ten-inch-circumference nylon lines were then passed by crane down to the supply vessel. Making fast was a tricky and dangerous job, especially in bad weather, as we didn't have the power or the big thrusters near the bow and stern that they have on these types of vessels nowadays. With modern rig tenders the thrusters can be controlled in conjunction with the main engines, either manually or in the automatic mode, relying on GPS. In auto mode a vessel can hold its position, hands off, but if one of our ships were to touch this rig, it would be referred to as a collision and, offshore in the usual sea and swell, that is exactly what it would be, with ensuing damage both to rig and vessel. Even a dent to the rig would be colossal, resulting in surveys, down-time and so on.

Our two supply vessels had long, low afterdecks that took up two-thirds of their length. The deck's forward end housed the tow winch, which comprised two drums, one wrapped with over two thousand feet of two-and-one-quarter-inch galvanized wire for towing and the other with a shorter work wire for picking up and setting the rig's anchors. Under the deck were the fresh water and fuel tanks holding a total of 150,000 gallons. We pumped the majority of the fresh water to the rig where they used a lot of the water and some of the diesel oil to mix with the barite to form mud for drilling and cement to cap the drill holes. The diesel fuel was for both our use and the rig's. Often we carried portable tanks on deck loaded with barite and this was also pumped up to the rig. We had a walk-in freezer and cooler for food supplies and carried pallets of bagged concrete and general cargo on deck. Every trip there were lengths of drill-pipe and steel casing used for the drilling. These were quite tricky to discharge as, even after intentionally giving the ship a list by transferring water ballast, the pipe and casing would shift and often start to roll on the deck as the ship was continuously tossing in the swell.

As these vessels were a combination of many things, they lacked the perfections of a vessel designed for one specific purpose. They were owned by an American company and were actually replicas of the newer rig tenders they were using in the Gulf of Mexico at that time. But the company's experience in this sort of work was limited to the Gulf area where the general sea conditions are much more placid and the depths shallower. In the event of a hurricane warning the rigs there were apparently abandoned. In fact, at that time offshore drilling in waters such as ours on the West Coast was just in its infancy.

When towing the *Sedco*, the *Gulf Joan*, which was a conventional tug, always towed from the centre tow position on the forward leg of the rig. The two rig-tenders had to tow from the forward leg, too—usually from the crown of the anchors seated on the rig—but on either side of the *Gulf Joan*. This meant that we were towing at an angle, and for best efficiency this angle was decreased as much as possible. However, for safety we had to keep a considerable distance away from the centre tow vessel. This resulted in the tow line leading over the side of our bulwarks near the stern, so it was impossible to use tow pins or any sort of hold-down gear designed to prevent the tow line from chafing. We would look at the *Gulf Joan* with envy. They had their tow line leading directly off the centre of the stern, held in place between two tow pins and secured with a hold-down clamp. Our line led over the side at a sharp angle and with just the slightest movement sparks would fly. When we used the radiophone to inform our shore office of the problem and the threat that the line would snap, they replied that we should use the mattresses from our bunks between the tow line and bulwarks, a remark that confirmed our suspicion that the company had never operated in these conditions. Of course, in just one swipe of the tow line sliding along the bulwarks, a mattress would be torn to shreds. We had a few scraps of steel plate that the engineers cut up and welded to create various types of chafing gear, but none of them worked adequately as they would twist around and bend or get sheared off. We had to either take in or let out the line by just a few feet every half-hour or so and continually grease the area.

These tows could take a day or weeks, depending on the location, and our speed varied from almost zero in severe weather to rarely more than about three knots. I recall that while doing similar work off the coast of Newfoundland, the other two rig tenders broke their towlines, and with just ourselves attached to the tow we went backwards for almost a week while towing against a big storm. During these tows, whoever was on watch in our wheelhouse spent most of his time looking down at the afterdeck with his eyes fixed on the towline.

Normally we worked week-on/week-off, with two separate crews for each vessel. However, when working anchors and moving the rig we doubled up on the crew. Then the days-off crew was called back, and everyone except the masters worked six hours on/six hours off. One skipper was at the controls and the other worked as pusher or foreman on deck. It meant long hours around the clock and then some.

The most dangerous job was the setting and, particularly, the retrieving of the rig's anchors whenever it was due to be moved to a new location. There were nine of them, fifteen tons each, and sometimes they would attach another ten-ton anchor just behind, which they called piggy-backing. The anchor locations were determined by hi-fix Decca, which relied on two portable land stations being set up prior to a rig move, and when doing the move, an operator who ran the Decca electrical equipment was on board each vessel. On the west coast off Ucluelet, I recall the positions being 1,900 feet out from the rig's three corners. A two-inch diameter cable or wire was permanently attached to the crown of each anchor. Once the anchor was set, we would disconnect this work wire at our end and attach a yellow, steel, cylindrical buoy about five by eight feet. The rig would then tension up on the chain but, if the anchor did not grab on the bottom, we would have to pick it up and go through the procedure again.

Retrieving the anchors was more hazardous. We lassoed the floating buoy with a three-quarter-inch-diameter wire, dragged the anchor over our stern, then attached our work-wire to the wire running down to the anchor. Generally the anchor was well-buried in the bottom, and with just a little strain on the winch we would try and unseat it, but it often took a long time before the anchor flukes

On June 3, 1979, the *Sedco 135F* was drilling a well for PEMEX, the state-owned Mexican petroleum company, when the well suffered a blowout. The decision was made to pull the drill string and plug the well. However, without the hydrostatic pressure of the mud column, oil and gas were able to flow unrestricted to the surface where they ignited and engulfed the *Sedco 135F* in flames. The rig collapsed and sank onto the seabed, littering it with large debris such as the rig's derrick and three thousand metres of pipe. By now the well was flowing at the rate of thirty thousand barrels a day [one barrel equals 159 litres], and two relief wells were drilled to relieve the pressure. The well was finally killed on March 23, 1980, nine months after the blowout.

This accident caused the biggest single spill ever, with an estimated 3.5 million barrels of oil released. Nearly five hundred aerial missions were flown to spray dispersants over the oil-covered water, but the prevailing winds blew it ashore along the US coast, causing extensive damage, especially in Texas. Fortunately, there were no fatalities in this accident.

would loosen their grip. With our relatively low 2,600 horsepower and the tremendous weight of chain, each link weighing well over one hundred pounds, it was a struggle to drag the anchors out to these positions. Nowadays, a similar rig-tender would have four times the horsepower of the *Min Tide*. We could not put too much strain on the wire as an extra big swell could easily cause it to snap. This is a different procedure from a normal ship at anchor where, as the anchor is heaved in, the ship moves ahead until it comes over top of it. The rig had to remain in position because the other eight anchors were running out in all directions. A fouled anchor meant hauling it over the stern of the rig tender and freeing the tangled wire from the flukes. Once everything was okay, we would lower the anchor over the stern a few feet and the rig would then haul it in.

We had a young crew, and their eagerness to do the job was never in question, but picking up anchors and untangling the two-inch wire wrapped around the flukes entailed long hours, sometimes a full day on one anchor, weather permitting. During this work it was always with the stern to the sea and swell, and the sea would often crash over the stern like breakers rolling in on a West Coast beach. Occasionally wires would break, and this would be followed by the tedious chore of grappling for the anchor chain and then continuing to retrieve. From the skipper's perspective, looking down without being able to communicate and seeing one or more crew members working in the bight of a wire that had the potential to snap was probably the most nerve-wracking experience of these vessels' whole operation.

On these vessels, the ten-inch circumference of the nylon tie-up lines to the rig was significant. When towing, we used a similar sized line as a spring or tension absorber between the actual towline and the crown of the anchor from which we towed. The anchor was seated "home" on the rig's pontoon at the foot of each leg. When offshore, this part of the rig was well below water level and you could not physically see the anchor. One time we were trying to lift the anchor over the stern and the nylon line stretched to such a point that it was like a length of hard steel. It suddenly snapped and, like a rubber band with the speed of a bullet, whipped the wheelhouse, smashed and badly damaged the lifeboat that was secured thwartships aft of the wheelhouse. It just missed the other skipper where he was standing at the outside controls and went between the two crew members who were standing on the other side of him. Had it hit one of us, we would have been split down the middle. One other time a grappling iron weighing about half a ton flipped off the chain and hit a seaman, knocking him down with two of its four prongs straddling his body. Had a prong hit him directly that would have been the end. As I recall he did suffer some injury and had to be sent ashore. He suffered some paralysis for a while but eventually recovered. He was extremely lucky.

Lee Slind, the geologist, describes the disappointing end of the program:

We drilled nine exploration wells during 1968—three in the Tofino Basin and six in the Queen Charlotte Basin. They were all abandoned because we did not find oil or gas in sufficiently producible quantities. The following year saw the completion of two more wells in the Tofino Basin and the last two Hecate Strait tests. All were dry and were abandoned. Although the company realized that the Canadian West Coast offshore was in its early stage of exploration, they decided that the results of these two years of furious drilling should be digested before a new round of work was considered. In 1969 the *Sedco 135F* was released to Shell International and the exploration operation wound down. Shell subsequently had discussions with other companies for joint operations in the area, but permission to drill has been withheld by the Canadian government. The West Coast offshore lands remain "under moratorium." No exploration is allowed, especially drilling, and land obligations are suspended until the moratorium is lifted.

Glossary

ARPA—Automatic Radar Plotting Aid.

beachcomber—a person licensed to salvage logs that have broken loose from log booms.

boomsticks—see sidesticks.

bridles—cable or chain, usually with an eye in each end, used for towing barges or logs to give equal pull on each side and make the barges tow in a straight line.

bulwark—the ship's side above the deck level.

caulk boots—(pronounced cork boots) protective boots fitted with "caulks" or small spikes on the soles to reduce slipping when working on log booms.

Davis raft—a forty-metre-long mat of logs woven together with steel cables; the logs were piled on in layers and the entire raft then wrapped securely with cable. Each raft contained about one million board feet.

deadhead—1) a submerged log that could be a danger to shipping. 2) a situation where a pilot stays on board a ship to the next port, even though his services are no longer needed.

double falls block—used on fishing trollers, it is composed of two wooden blocks, each with two pulleys, one attached to the derrick, the other hanging free on the end of the ropes threaded through them with a hook on the end of the block; a rope runs through the blocks to the winch.

dozers—very small one-man tugboats that assist in moving logs in the water.

dry suit—a watertight suit with a hood; it totally covers the diver's body, keeping it dry and trapping air inside.

fench up—the anchor starts catching bottom.

gimbals—a contrivance of rings and pivots for keeping instruments aboard ship in a horizontal position.

GPS—Global Positioning System is a satellite system sending radio signals used to navigate, enabling anyone who owns a GPS receiver to know their location twenty-four hours a day and to plot a course between two points.

gurdies—spools that hold the trolling lines on fishboats.

gyro or gyrocompass—a navigational compass containing a gyroscope rotor that measures the direction of true north along the surface of the earth.

Kort nozzle—a non-steering nozzle with a rudder behind it.

Loran—a device by which a navigator can locate his position by determining the time displacement between radio signals from two known stations.

old man—the popular term used to refer to a ship's captain.

penboards—horizontal boards inside a fishboat's hold that fit into the slots in the vertical stanchions and provide divisions in the hold to keep the fish from shifting.

ro-ro vessel—a roll-on, roll-off vessel with a ramp that allows wheeled cargo to be driven on and off.

scotchman—an inflatable buoy, usually red, attached to a cable, often used to mark an underwater location.

shackle—a device attached to the anchor chain every fifteen fathoms to indicate the length of the chain that has been let out. One link on each side of the shackle is painted white for the first shackle, two links for the second, etc.

sidesticks or **boomsticks**—logs, usually sixty-six feet long, with a hole drilled in either end; they are connected with boom chains to enclose the perimeter of a log boom.

stanchions—vertical boards dividing the sections of a fishboat's hold and supporting the penboards.

telegraph—a system for transmitting messages to the engine room.

tender—1) the person who oversees a diving boat and the breathing equipment while a diver is under the water. 2) a ship that provides a larger one with supply stores or conveys passengers to it.

waiting weather—waiting in a sheltered location until the heavy weather eases

wetsuit—a body suit made of neoprene rubber worn to keep the diver warm; it allows a small amount of water to leak through at the neck, ankle and wrist openings and is kept warm by body heat.

wheel—the propeller or the steering control.

wire—steel cable.

Index